Advanced Praise for

The Modern Woman

"Trez Ibrahim's book The Modern Woman brilliantly describes four feminine archetypes within every woman, and how to understand which ones are driving us and why... and how much power they have to wreak havoc on our self-esteem, health, and relationships – or transform them into the life we desire. I love the simplicity and clarity of this idea, and saw myself and all the women I know in it. This book is full of so much wisdom and practical advice. I loved it."

— **Carol Allen, Vedic Astrologer and relationship coach, author of Love is in the Stars – the Wise Woman's Astrological Guide to Men.**

THE *Modern* WOMAN

DISCOVER YOUR INNER SWEET, SEXY, BAD*SS QUEEN

TREZ IBRAHIM

Silver Laurel Publishing House
California

Trez Ibrahim
Silver Laurel Publishing House
360 East First St., #426
Tustin, CA 92780

Warning – Disclaimer

The purpose of this book is to educate and entertain. The author and/or publisher shall have neither liability nor responsibility to anyone with respect to any loss or damage caused, or alleged to be caused, directly or indirectly by the information contained in this book.

CONTENTS

Dedication 1

Introduction 2

PART I

The Modern Goddess

1. The Journey 5
2. The Awakening 17

PART II

The Sweet Mother

3. The Mother 27
4. The Inner Mother 39
5. Breaking the Binds 45
6. Self Worth 53
7. A Mother's Gift 64
8. Gifting and Receiving 73
9. Your Body 78
10. You Are Not Broken 85

PART III

The Sexy Playmate

11. The Playmate 92
12. Your Body Beautiful 96
13. Self Care 104

14. Flow 109
15. Her Joy 115
16. Sexual Trauma 123
17. Let Her Out to Play 134

PART IV

The Bad*ass CEO

18. The CEO 139
19. Power 148
20. Boundaries 158
21. Speak Up Darling 164
22. Your Domain 168
23. Money and Power 175

PART V

The Queenly High Priestess

24. The High Priestess 184
25. Graceful Entry 194
26. Quiet Strength 205
27. True Power 218
28. Healing and Growing 229

Conclusion 237
Afterword 242
Acknowledgements 245
About the Author 247

Dedication

This book is dedicated to my beloved parents. To my mom, who taught me the power of unconditional love and the importance of nurturing others. And to my dad, who showed me what it means to be adored and cherished as a woman. Thank you for your unwavering support, encouragement, and for being the guiding lights in my life. You have instilled in me the values of strength, grace, and resilience that have shaped me into the woman I am today. I am forever grateful for the love and inspiration you have given me. This book is a tribute to you, and to all the women who strive to awaken their inner sweet, sexy, badass queen.

Introduction

Within every woman are four powerful archetypes, each a magnificent facet of her being, yearning to be expressed, cherished, and harmoniously woven together. These archetypes are the keys to unlocking a life of profound meaning, happiness, and success. However, when these archetypal forces are out of balance, suppressed or neglected, they wreak havoc on her life, creating chaos in her world, and leaving behind a trail of exhaustion, burnout, and despair.

This is a tale of transformation, the metamorphosis of a woman who once unknowingly walked the path of imbalance and disarray. This woman was me. Unbeknownst to me, I had become a mere shadow of my true self, my life teetering on the brink of collapse. My marriage crumbled, my motherhood faltered, my career deteriorated, and I found solace in the comfort of food, gaining a hundred pounds in the process.

My transformation was through the gift of archetypes. You may be asking, can the key to unlocking our potential truly lie within the simplicity of archetypes? Yes, these timeless constructs, as ancient as humanity itself, possess a universal resonance, intricately woven into the fabric of universal consciousness. I invite you to uncover the superpowers that reside within your very being. Embrace the opportunity to become the most integrated, whole, and greatest version of yourself, reaching the height of your potential.

I extend a heartfelt invitation for you to follow along with me on this remarkable journey of transformation, as I share my passage from the depths of despair to the invaluable lessons learned and ultimately to the beautiful, fabulous life I now proudly call mine. Along the way, I have guided countless women in harnessing the extraordinary power of archetypes to elevate their lives to unparalleled heights of beauty and fulfillment.

Together, let us embark on this fun and fabulous journey, diving into the realms of archetypes as we unleash our innermost strengths and become the most integrated, whole, and ascended version of ourselves possible.

Are you ready to unleash your inner goddess and become a confident, radiant woman? Are you ready to feel whole, fulfilled, and connect to your femininity, power, and grace? This book is about you, and the journey to fully embody the 4 Feminine Archetypes - The Mother, the Playmate, the CEO, and the High Priestess.

I invite you to step into the world of the empowered woman. In this book, we will uncover the secrets of embodying these four Feminine Archetypes and discover a new level of wholeness and fulfillment. Say goodbye to exhaustion and depletion, and become a Sweet, Sexy, Badass Queen in every aspect of your life. Own your power and grace as you soar to new heights of success, stand up for yourself, and make your mark on the world. Embrace your femininity, feel beautiful, sexy, and alive, and connect to the soft, gentle part of yourself that longs for love and connection. This is your moment to shine and claim your place as the confident, radiant woman you were born to be. Get ready to ignite the fire within and transform You with this life-changing guide.

PART I

The *Modern* Goddess

One

THE JOURNEY

"Life's journey is not always easy, but with every obstacle we face, we have the opportunity to tap into our inner strength and embrace our power as modern women. We are inspired by the lessons of the amazing women who came before us, and we continue to pave the way for those who will follow."

LESSONS LEARNED FROM BRAZILIAN WOMEN

Have you ever envied a woman who seems to have it all? From the luxurious Chanel bag to the stunning Versace outfit, her beauty and confidence shine brighter than the stars. With her handsome companion by her side, she glides into a room and commands attention with her grace and warmth. But it's not just her outer appearance that sets her apart. Her success is palpable in the way she walks, with a proud stature and a commanding presence. Envision yourself as that woman, poised and in control. This book is your invitation to unlock the secrets of embodying the ultimate confident, successful woman.

Years ago, I was surrounded by a group of these seemingly perfect women.

I found myself in the company of a group of seemingly impeccable women. At a conference in San Diego, I was introduced to a Brazilian woman who radiated a mesmerizing beauty that instantly drew me in. I was enchanted by her charm, charisma, and her radiant essence, and I was grateful to be welcomed into her circle of friends. Unlike some female groups I had encountered in the past, this group was free of cliquishness, catty behavior, or competition.

One evening, this woman invited me to join her and her friends for dinner. When I arrived at the hotel lobby to meet her friends, I was pleased to learn that they were all from Brazil as well. As I was introduced to each of them, I was struck by their indescribable beauty and radiance. Despite not having any particularly outstanding physical features or being supermodels, their attire and accessories were impeccable and captured my admiration.

Physically they were stunning, although from simply a physical perspective, there wasn't anything spectacular about their looks. There were no features that stood out. They weren't supermodels; nor did they have perfect, slim bodies. They were, however, beautifully clothed and accessorized, and everything about their physical appearance looked impeccable. What was truly remarkable about this group of women was their magnetic energy and their ability to connect with each other in such an alluring manner. As soon as I was greeted with a warm embrace and a kiss on the cheek, I felt like the center of attention, as if their complete focus was on me alone. They exuded a nurturing quality and a kind heartedness that made everyone around them feel at ease.

These women were also powerful and self-assured. They were confident, and it was evident that they would not tolerate anyone who crossed their boundaries. Over dinner, I listened as they shared stories and was in awe of their strength in handling challenging situations. They were successful women, with some owning their own companies and others being entrepreneurs and executives.

I noticed, as the evening wore on, that even though they could be outgoing, vivacious and dynamic, there was still something gentle, centered and grounded within them.

As I watched these women, I had the same thought that you might be having now: I wish I could have what they have, or even just a small part of it. At the time, I was going through a difficult period in my life. I had recently gone through a messy divorce after being married for seven years, and I was taking care of my infant alone. I weighed over 200 pounds, precisely 236 pounds, and felt unhappy with myself. I was exhausted, felt hopeless, and lacked confidence in my abilities. I felt betrayed, lost, alone, and completely disconnected from myself. I no longer knew who I was, what I wanted, or how to feel good about myself. All I wanted was to escape from my body and the constant darkness that surrounded me. I was searching for a ray of hope, something to help me out of this deep hole and give me the strength to keep going. That's when I came across these women, who seemed to be the answer to my prayers. Maybe they held the key to reconnect with my core, to feel beautiful and light again, and to find the courage to face my life head-on.

I became immensely curious about how these women radiated such desirable qualities. Initially, I found myself lamenting my upbringing, wishing I had been born to Brazilian parents. Perhaps then, I too could have lived a life like theirs. As I pondered my predicament, I realized that since I couldn't change my birth, moving to Brazil might be the next best thing. Just being around these women could be enough to transform me into a replica of their confident and composed selves. I had convinced myself that their charm and magnetism were exclusive gifts to Brazilian women.

But deep down, I knew that relocating was not the answer. After spending time with a few of them, I discovered that they were just as flawed as I was. Underneath the stylish clothes, impeccably manicured nails, and social finesse, lay failed marriages, financial struggles, and a profound sense of self-doubt. Despite this, my fascination with their demeanor persisted. I wanted it all, what I saw in them and more. How could I learn to be beautiful, confident, resilient, and alluring both inside and out? How could I feel at ease with myself, be successful in my relationships, career, and finances, and look forward to each new day with excitement?

Hence, my journey out of the abyss began.

Let's start at the very beginning of my journey to discover what it means to be a woman. I was just seven years old when Nadia, a friend of the family, came to visit during the holidays. Nadia was simply breathtaking. From the moment she stepped into our home, I was captivated by her charm and wanted to be by her side for the entire celebration. Despite my clingy behavior, Nadia never made me feel like a pesky kid. She was radiant with her long, shiny black hair and impeccably dressed in gorgeous clothing. Her laughter was like music to my ears and her every move oozed grace and poise.

One thing Nadia did that surprised me was to encourage me to help my mother in the kitchen. This was something I would never do on my own. I despised working in the kitchen or anywhere else in the home. As soon as Mom began any chores, I was out of the house faster than a bullet. But, with Nadia by my side, it felt like a natural and loving experience. Nadia made it seem effortless and enjoyable, unlike the hard labor I thought it was.

Nadia quickly became my role model. I wanted to be just like her when I grew up. Little did I know that years later, when I found myself lost and searching for meaning, Nadia's memory would pop into my mind. It coincided with my meeting the Brazilian women who exuded the same irresistible qualities as Nadia. I knew I had to learn more about what made them so magnetic, successful, and attractive.

And so began my journey of discovery. It led me to uncover the "secret" to their appeal. I discovered a wealth of knowledge from beautiful, smart, brilliant, and spiritual women. This journey taught me how to rediscover myself and find my place in the world.

LOSING OURSELVES

These are exciting times for women. Today, we have many choices and far more opportunities than our grandmothers or even our mothers ever had. We can work if we choose to, achieve financial security, have children with or without a partner, and travel anywhere our hearts desire around the world. There are few limitations, at least in most developed countries, on what we can achieve, where we can go, what we can do, or the decisions we can make. We have access to earning our own money and gaining security, power, prestige, and even fame. The door to countless opportunities has opened. Yet, many women on this quest for a fulfilling life find themselves tired, worn-out, and even disheartened.

Women want to have, be, and do it all. It's about time, I get it. We have figured out how men find success and try to emulate the men. Yet, in this attempt at living "on your own terms", and wanting to thrive in what was once exclusively a man's world, some women find that they are losing themselves.

Women have learned to create safety, financial security, and independence by stepping into their doing, goal-oriented, and achieving "masculine" energy. We have learned how to make things happen by our own efforts, hard work and grind. What was once the role of the men in women's lives, we have taken on for ourselves. We added to our plate, accomplishing, achieving and taking care of everyone else's needs, and were not quite sure what to do with the extra workload. Women's liberation freed us to explore the other side of our innate selves and while this is admirable and a powerful step on the road to evolution, it has had its drawbacks. We neglected our greatest gifts as women to embody both the masculine and feminine energies and instead of a marriage of the two, we created a divorce, and in the split of assets, most women opted for the masculine.

Most women have given up their inherent feminine energy and failed to connect the best of both worlds. They did what they had to do to survive. They accomplished, they achieved, they got the big corner offices, and the big jobs with the big raises. But they lost their feminine spirit; and for many, their health and relationships. Most successful women feel they have to choose between their career and love, and most often choose career with the financial security it brings. Then they find themselves burned out, stressed, lost and alone. And they ignored what their heart and soul was yearning for; wholeness, love, and freedom.

Most women mistakenly thought they had to choose between the masculine and the feminine. I am going to show you how you can now embody both. This book is my attempt to show you how you can create success in your life while still feeling whole, fulfilled and complete, so you can thrive exquisitely on your own terms. You will discover how to embrace your graceful feminine energy while still maintaining your power and independence in today's world. Feminine power is so much more than copying masculine power. I coach women all the time. These are successful women, who have lost sight of their core, what they truly desire deep within, and who they are as women. Through our work, they have learned to embrace all of who they are and create more success for themselves while living a beautiful life surrounded by the support they have always longed for.

This is my goal for you. That if you truly embody these principles, you will reconnect with your true essence, feel sexy and beautiful, create success and fulfillment, have supportive loving relationships with people that give as much as you, and live a life beyond your wildest dreams.

This is part "how to" book, part personal stories of my life and the lives of some incredible women I have had the privilege of working with, and part recognizing and applying what you see in your life.

For the men reading this, I want to offer a big Thank You. Thank you for taking the time to understand the plight of women in your life, to get to know how you can support the women you love in reclaiming their own femininity. Thank you for supporting them in feeling safe to be who they are, so they can do what comes natural to them, be the container of love in your life. As you read this book, you will gain a deeper insight into how women think and how they feel. You will acquire an understanding of how they can regain their own balance so you can have the powerful, loving relationship which you so desire. In these ever changing times, please know, we are learning, we are growing and we are evolving. We are learning about our roles, about what we desire and about how we can live a life full of joy; a life of our dreams.

Thank you for joining us.

This is a journey; a journey of becoming, and a journey of giving ourselves the best possibilities and opportunities to step into our power, our beauty, our bliss and our grace.

BREAKING FREE

I loved being a girl. I loved everything about it. At 4 years old, I had everything girly: pink blankets, pink pillows and princess vanity mirrors. I loved dressing in pink clothing, raiding my mom's closet and putting on her high heels and lipstick, baking brownies in my own easy bake oven and styling Barbie's hair.

As I grew older, and wiser, I quickly learned being a girl was weak. Girls didn't get to do the cool things boys got to do. Girls were supposed to be quiet, clean, and take care of everyone else. Girls were expected to sit quietly and coyly by their parents' side while the boys got to be rambunctious, play full out and roll around in the mud. Boys got to take risks, play outside without supervision and be celebrated for being silly and obnoxious.

I envied the freedom and perks boys had. I was proud to call myself my father's daughter and I wanted to be him. I wanted to be just like the man that had the freedom, the power, the achievements and the praise. My father went to work, worked hard, paid the bills, made final decisions in the household and was the man of the house. With that came respect. I learned early on not to question dad. Dad was the leader of the house and commanded applause after every accomplishment, big or small. It didn't matter if he bought a new car or carried in the mail.

My mother, by the way, also worked hard and made money. She worked 9 to 5, just like my dad. Oh, and when she came home, while my dad parked his weary body in front of the TV, my mother began her second job. She began to do the laundry, make dinner, take care of the kids, clean the house and do the dishes. She may have been able to finally sit on the couch by my dad at some point at the end of the night just before bedtime, but those are faint memories.

No thank you! That was not the path I wanted to follow. While she took ownership of her traditional feminine role of caring for the home and her family, along with the new male role of working outside the home without hesitation, I wanted no part of it. I saw my choice between working my butt off all day and night, not getting any recognition, versus working during the day, and being the hero at night. I chose the latter.

For me, that meant owning my new role, the role the 80's, women's liberation and the feminist movement promised. This new role allowed me to choose another way, denying my feminine and choosing to be just like a guy. I can wear the pants, compete with men and make my own decisions. I can even have a child without a man and can live in a man's world just fine. I, like most other women of that era, never really thought through where it would lead me.

Having been the only daughter of overprotective parents, my brother was forced to watch over me. To my brother's dismay, he had no choice but to lug his little sister alongside him and take her to all his activities. That was just fine with me. I wanted to be one of the boys. I skate-boarded down the hill we lived on, climbed the hills by our house and rode bikes along the river bed. I was very competitive with the boys and my motto was "everything you can do, I can do better". Although I didn't always beat the bigger and stronger boys, I was proud that I had played in the same league as them. And the funny thing is, I got praise for being competitive, strong and independent.

Although it temporarily made me feel better and hid my insecurities around being just a girl with all its limitations, as you can probably guess, this competitive nature didn't go over too well in my first major relationship. It began the week we came home from our honeymoon. The dishes began to pile up lurkingly in the sink. Soon, they were overflowing onto the counter. I pretended not to notice. There was no way I was going to do the dishes. I would not follow my mother's footsteps and become a slave of the home. Of course, as the man, my new husband had equal conviction and refused to do any household chores. Needless to say, that marriage didn't last long.

I got married right out of college. Determined not to repeat the pattern, I refused to do any cleaning around the house, and living with a man who was clueless about household chores, this led to many fights. I had a mind of my own and can say and do what I want, when I want. I made my own money and was able to take care of all my financial needs without any help. I was an independent strong woman who can take care of herself. I can make my own decisions and did not need permission from a man to go after what I want. I was efficient, smart and capable. I can always tell him the fastest way to get somewhere, and if he was lost, was never shy about telling him he made a wrong turn. After all, I can speak my mind and own my truth, no matter the cost. Decisions, well, I can make my own and of course correct him when he made the wrong decisions. Appreciation? Why would I appreciate anything he does when I work just as hard, or in my mind, even harder? I wasn't timid about correcting him in public and questioned everything he said. Just a few short years later, I found myself heartbroken and dismayed when our marriage ended.

I was a hard worker, putting in long and arduous hours in order to overachieve and prove myself at every opportunity. I was able to successfully run a business while also volunteering and serving as an Assistant Director of a large non-profit organization. Through my dedication and hard work, I was able to exceed all of my goals and build a department that received national recognition. I was proud of my accomplishments and felt like a true badass who could overcome any challenge. As a leader, I set high standards for myself and my team and was able to inspire my team to become strong leaders themselves.

However, after several years of pushing myself to the limit, I began to feel exhausted, burnt out, and depleted. Despite my best efforts, I couldn't seem to shake off these feelings of emptiness and despair. I was tired and felt lost and alone, but I refused to give up hope. I knew that there had to be another way to live my life that didn't involve sacrificing my own well-being for the sake of my career and accomplishments.

I embarked on a journey of self-discovery after going through a difficult period following my divorce. I yearned to understand who I truly was, where I belonged, and what it meant to be a whole and balanced woman. At the time, I felt pulled in many different directions and torn apart. I longed to feel beautiful, as I had gained weight and felt worthless and unattractive. I was a single mother caring for my infant son while also trying to rebuild my life after leaving a successful business I had co-owned with my ex-husband. I aspired to achieve success in the workplace without working myself to exhaustion. My daily routine left me drained, and I desperately needed to find balance, peace of mind, and a new way of living. I realized that I could no longer continue as I had been.

As women, we juggle many roles and responsibilities, including being wives, mothers, therapists, nutritionists, business owners, and employees. We manage households and wear multiple hats within each area of our lives. We're expected to step into the roles of mom, dad, nurse, counselor, teacher, problem solver, manager, advisor, judge, jury, and lawyer, making countless decisions each day. With the various aspects and dimensions of our lives, the question becomes: how can we balance it all and maintain our sanity, let alone find fulfillment? How can we integrate everything so that we feel empowered as women instead of depleted at the end of the day?

UNRAVELING THE MYSTERY OF ARCHETYPES

I embarked on a quest to uncover the essence of the women I admired. I understood that their unique qualities were not solely determined by genetics, nationality, or cultural background, whether they were Nadia or Brazilian goddesses. I yearned to emulate these women, to embody their admirable traits and make them my own. I delved into extensive research, voraciously studied various topics, attended numerous workshops, and closely observed women to identify the factors that rendered them captivating, content, and exceptional. I began to discern and appreciate the attributes and characteristics of other women that attracted me and other individuals to them.

As these women entered a room, I analyzed the energy, characteristics, behaviors, and identities that illuminated the space. In my search for answers, I stumbled upon the concept of archetypes. This led me to the works of Carl Jung and Joseph Campbell. Jung, a Swiss psychiatrist, believed that archetypes were universal, innate models of human behavior and personality passed down through generations. Campbell, an American mythologist, lecturer, and writer, studied and wrote about mythological, religious, and psychological archetypes, applying these concepts to modern life.

These archetypes are within all of us, waiting to be consciously accessed, adapted, and assimilated into our lives. They represent aspects of our being that we can actively exhibit or that may lay dormant, waiting for the right moment to awaken.

As I navigated through the maze of concepts and philosophies, I sought to simplify these ideas, to piece them together, and make them tangible. As a teacher, I love taking complex ideas and breaking them down into practical solutions that are easy to implement for quick and lasting change.

My desire was to create a roadmap to empower individuals to access their full potential and create a fulfilling life. A puzzle so clear that if there was something missing in one's life, they would know exactly where to go and how to fit the missing piece in, feeling powerful, connected, alive, and beautiful.

Join me on this journey of self-discovery and transformation. Let us unlock our true potential and embody the archetypes that lay within us. A journey that will be both fun and life-changing.

Two

THE AWAKENING

"Awakening the modern goddess within is not about perfection, but rather a journey of self-discovery, self-love, and self-acceptance. It's about embracing your unique strengths, honoring your true essence, and living your life with purpose and passion."

AWAKENING THE FOUR FEMININE ARCHETYPES

In my quest for understanding the multifaceted dimensions of womanhood that I yearned to embody, I had an epiphany. It all came down to four divine archetypes, each representing a distinct aspect of the feminine essence - the Mother, the Playmate, the CEO, and the High Priestess. These archetypes, when synergistically balanced within us, help us unlock the inner sanctum of our soul, and unleash the goddess within. These powerful four Archetypes, or Feminine Types, dancing in harmony with each other, allow us as women to discover our Inner Sweet, Sexy, Badass Queen. We all have these. We all have the ability to bring out these characteristics within each of us and unleash the goddess within... This is our true nature. This is not about trying to become something or someone you are not. This is about bringing out the best within each and every one of us.

In every woman, these archetypes lie, dormant or awakened, representing the various facets of her personality, character, and behavior. We must embark on a journey of self-discovery, to unlock these archetypes, and bring forth the inherent qualities that have been latent within us, waiting to be unleashed. By doing so, we can explore the very depths of our true selves, and access the wisdom and power that reside within.

These archetypes are more than just mere personifications of personality traits. They are the embodiment of the essence of the feminine, and by embracing each one, we can fully awaken to our own divine power. But in our pursuit of these archetypes, we must also understand how we can become imbalanced or misaligned in our lives, and work to reintegrate them in a holistic, organic manner, and develop the ability to call upon that which we need or desire every day, in every moment that we choose.

This book is not just a guide to the four feminine archetypes, but a journey of self-discovery, empowerment, and transformation. We will explore how these archetypes manifest in every aspect of our lives, from our relationships to our careers, our spirituality to our parenting. By embracing the divine feminine within, we can unlock the limitless potential that has been waiting for us all along.

THE JOURNEY OF SELF DISCOVERY

In my workshops and with my personal VIP clients, I guide them on a journey of self-discovery and connection to their inner Selves with a capital "S". For women, this connection is vital to navigate the demands and expectations of the physical world and maintain their sanity. It is within this inner sanctuary where our truth lies and where we can find the answers that guide us. Trusting your inner voice, your inner truth will never steer you wrong, and it knows where you should go and what you should do.

To embark on this journey, we must first take a quick inventory of our current lives. We need to know where we are to get to where we want to go. In the following exercise, we will explore how the four divine archetypes manifest in our lives. Don't overthink it or analyze it, but approach it with a playful energy that you had as a child. Bring forth your inner Playmate, and allow the process to unfold naturally and organically. Trust what you receive, and keep a journal handy to jot down any thoughts or insights you receive.

We will begin with an opening meditation to identify which feminine archetype you tend to live from throughout the majority of your day and life. Most women lean towards one or two ways of being or acting consistently, and we will explore which archetype is a bit neglected and out of balance in your life. By discovering which feminine type you embody and which needs attention, we can begin to balance and integrate them to unleash the goddess within. Let's embark on this transformative journey together.

Visit my website at www.SweetSexyBadassQueen.com to listen to the recording of this visualization exercise or you can follow the steps here.

Read through the entire exercise first to get an idea of what to expect then close your eyes and go through the steps. It is important that you do this in a quiet, centered, meditative state in order to access your inner truth.

MEDITATION EXERCISE

Begin by making yourself comfortable in your chair with your feet flat on the ground and arms and legs uncrossed. Ensure a full, unrestricted flow throughout your body and sit up straight. Gently close your eyes and take a couple of long, deep cleansing breaths. Breathe all the way into your body, from the top of your head down to the tips of your toes. Settle into your body and feel your skin enveloping it. Notice any sensations around your body.

Visualize a large coil of rope under your seat. Tie one end of the rope to the base of your spine, right at your seat, and attach an anchor to the other end of the rope. Release the anchor and allow it to fall towards the center of the planet. Watch as the rope uncoils, moving quickly and easily through your chair, into the ground and through all the layers of the earth. See the details of the rope connected to the base of your spine and the other end going down into the earth. Without any effort, watch it move down thousands of miles until it reaches the center of the planet. When you hear a little clink, you'll know you've arrived. You may also simply see the rope connected to the center of the earth.

If there's any slack in the rope, you can give it a little tug to straighten it out. Make sure that you're fully connected to the earth and present in your body.

Take a deep breath and release all the energy from the day. Let go of any tension, stress, and worries that are weighing you down. Release any energy that's no longer serving you and anything or anyone that's taking up space in your physical and energetic space. Let go of any conversations you're having in your head with other people and any items on your to-do list. If any people come to mind, simply greet them and allow them to slide down the grounding cord. If there are any men who may want your attention, let them know that this time is for you, and they can enjoy you later. If there are any women who are in competition with you, release them gently.

Allow yourself to get comfortable in this space, and after a few minutes, you may want to set the grounding cord on automatic release. This allows gravity to easily and effortlessly pull the energy that you're ready to release into the planet so that it can be recycled and sent back to where it belongs.

Imagine a four-leaf clover out in front of you. Watch that four-leaf clover and see all the details of it, the size, the color, the shape, the texture. Look at the four-leaf clover in three dimensions and admire what you created in your imagination. You are going to have that four-leaf clover represent each of the four Feminine Archetypes. We will pay attention to the Feminine Types, one by one. Notice what happens to the leaf as you say hello to each Feminine Archetype and notice how you bring those energies into the body. Notice how you are able to incorporate each type into your life and how strong or powerful that Feminine Type is in your life.

Look at the top right-hand corner of the four-leaf clover and allow that to represent your Mother archetype. How are you able to incorporate that Feminine archetype of being a Mother in your life currently? How much are you able to connect with people on a deep emotional level? To what extent are you connected to what others are thinking, how they are feeling, what it is they need? How in touch are you with that part of you that can heal others, maybe without them even asking, the part of you that can give to others, take care of others, nurture others and make them feel better? How willing are you to say Yes to others? How much do you love serving others? The Mother is also the part that can give to yourself, can nurture yourself, heal yourself, take care of yourself, connect with yourself emotionally and allow yourself to be vulnerable. It is in our vulnerability, being able to go to the depths of our emotions, that our power lies. How connected are you with your own needs? Notice what that leaf looks like? Is it frayed or frazzled? Does it look three-dimensional? What color is it? Is it vibrant and alive? How big and robust is it?

Move your attention down to the bottom right-hand leaf on that clover allowing that to represent your inner Playmate. This is the part of you that can enjoy life and feel bliss. This is the part of you that can laugh out loud and loves to have fun. This aspect of you loves having sex, loves being in groups of people, is flirtatious, and loves to dress in pretty clothes. How developed is the Playmate in your life? This is the inner three-year-old little girl that wore her mother's heels and red lipstick and walked through the house with a queen's stride. She paraded around like little Miss Universe. How much are you able to enjoy life, enjoy yourself, enjoy good food, and enjoy the wind in your hair? How sexy do you feel? How in touch are you with your sensuality, taking in everything that comes through the senses; the tastes, the smells, the sounds, and the feel of life? Do you enjoy intimacy, sensual and sexual pleasures and take every opportunity to seduce, tease and have fun with your partner? Do you enjoy sex or has it become a chore? Are you in touch with your outer beauty? Do you take time to take care of yourself, workout, get dressed up, pay attention to your health and wellness as well as your grooming, or have you let yourself physically go? Do you enjoy adventure and excitement or are you resigned to the mundane in life, doing the same thing day after day, simply going through the motions? Notice what that Playmate looks like. Notice what that leaf that represents the Playmate on that four leaf clover looks like.

Look at the bottom left leaf, allow that to represent the CEO feminine type. Notice the strength of your inner CEO. Are you able to get things done in the world? Do you feel accomplished and successful? Do you follow through on your word and complete what you begin? Do you procrastinate? Do you say No when you mean No or do you have a difficult time saying No to others? Do you say Yes to those things you are committed to and follow through as required? Are you able to stand up for yourself? Are you able to create things for yourself? Do you see the results that you desire in your life? Are you financially secure? Are you able to create prosperity for yourself, make things happen and get things done? Do you feel safe when you are out in the world? Are you able to set boundaries and stick with them? Do you feel in control or have you gone to the opposite extreme, trying to dominate over everyone and *everything in life? Do you feel as if you are making up for a lack of feeling in real control? Do you throw your weight around, are passive aggressive or belittle others in order to feel powerful? Do you feel like a "bi***" sometimes, overreacting to regain control? Allow that leaf to show you the state of the inner CEO in your life. It might be a strong leaf. It may be big and wide, It may be thin and frail, weak and small, or it might shrink. Simply take note of what it looks like.*

Move your attention to the top left-hand corner of that four-leaf clover and allow that to represent your High Priestess. How much of your High Priestess is active in your life? Do you have a daily spiritual practice? Do you feel connected to your essence? Do you feel connected to your source, divinity, that power within you that is always available and has the truth? Can you surrender to life or do you try to control everything? Do you enjoy your time with your inner Self, the quiet space connecting you with the deep core of who you are?

How often do you act and feel like a lady, that doesn't need to enter into a situation with brute strength, but rather can approach life with a calm gentleness? Are you polite, led by true integrity and deep core values? Do you maintain high standards for yourself and those around you? Are you in touch with the part of you that is respectful, soft-spoken? Do you exhibit mannerisms that are elegant? Can you surrender to experiences in your life? Do you elegantly glide into a room or do you trot? How much are you connected to that beauty within, the High Priestess that is beautiful simply by the light that she emanates? Have you resigned in life, allowing whatever happens to happen with no real connection? Are you flaky, a damsel in distress, faking spirituality or allow it to be led by the ego? Are you meditating all day waiting for the law of attraction to do its magic while you do nothing? How much of that High

Priestess is allowed in your life right now in the present moment, in present time? There is no need to fix anything, just notice, simply say hello.

Take one more glance at that four leaf clover and notice what all the leaves look like. The top right hand corner is the Mother, the bottom right is the Playmate and bottom left is the CEO and the top left is the High Priestess. Release the four leaf clover out of your space. Allow that to release down the grounding, into the earth and let it go. Let it move out of your space.

Now replenish your space. Imagine a big golden sun above your head. You can put a little driver's license size picture of yourself attached to a strong magnet in the center of that golden sun. This is your sun and you can call back your energy, your essence, and your beautiful colors back into it. Allow that picture to magnetize your essence into that golden sun from wherever you left it. Watch the golden sun get bigger and brighter as it fills up with all of your beautiful colors. When it is all filled up, you can start to bring that ball of golden light down from the top of the head, down your face, your neck, and start to fill up your entire body. Fill up your aura, that space around your body, with your energy. Feel that light move down your chest, your back, your torso, down to your hips. Continue down your thighs, and your legs. Watch that sun completely fill up all the spaces in your body and in your aura that you just created for yourself. Watch that continue down your ankles, your feet and send some of that down the grounding to validate the grounding cord.

The High Priestess loves this type of meditation. When you're all filled up, you can slowly open your eyes, stretch, bend over and stand up stretching your entire body. Validate the body. The Playmate wants to feel comfortable in her skin and loves to stretch and move.

YOUR AWAKENING JOURNAL

Take a moment to reflect and journal on your innermost self. Each leaf may look similar, yet each one is unique in its own way. As you observe, which leaf stands out to you as being the strongest?

In this moment, you are connecting with the energy of the High Priestess, the wise and intuitive Feminine archetype. It is through journaling and self-reflection that you can deepen this connection and truly understand how these archetypes play out in your life.

Take a moment to ponder the dominant force in your life - is it the nurturing Mother, the playful Playmate, the powerful CEO, or the intuitive High Priestess? Which of these Feminine archetypes takes a back seat in your life currently? What images, memories, thoughts, or emotions arise within you as you reflect upon this? Remember, this is a judgment-free zone. The first step towards transformation is simply becoming aware of your current situation. That's where journaling comes in - it is a powerful tool for gaining clarity and understanding your innermost thoughts and emotions.

As you continue on this journey, I encourage you to journal throughout your time reading this book. Take note of what resonates with you, the changes you'd love to make, and what you'd love to do more or less of. Take note of how each Feminine type plays out in your life and what is missing from your daily experience.

Now that you've gained an awareness of how you show up for yourself in your life, it's time to explore each of the four Feminine Types in greater detail. With this exploration, you'll uncover ways to embrace the Mother, Playmate, CEO, and High Priestess within you more powerfully, so that you can live a life of beauty, bliss, power, and grace. Are you ready to embark on this transformative journey?

Let's begin…

PART II

The Sweet *Mother*

Three

THE MOTHER

"Motherhood is the greatest thing and the hardest thing."
~ Ricki Lake ~

YOUR INNER MOTHER

In our journey to uncover the power of the Feminine, we begin with the first type: The Mother. Embodiment of this archetype is key, but what is the Mother exactly? What are her needs, and what happens when they are not met?

The Mother represents the sweet, caring aspect of the Feminine. She is in tune with the emotions, thoughts, and desires of others and loves to share. Driven by her emotional body, she is extremely intuitive and can anticipate the needs of others before they are even expressed. As a giver, caretaker, and nurturer, the Mother is a source of life, nourishment, and support. She gives unconditionally and is a fountain of love, patience, devotion, caring and unselfish acts. From children to extended family, friendships, and even work relationships, she is the keeper and protector of all forms of life.

It is important to note that every woman possesses this aspect of the Feminine, regardless of whether she has children or not. Generous with her energy, time, talents, and resources, the Mother is the one who takes care of those around her. Understanding and forgiving, she is highly attuned to the emotions and thoughts of others, connecting with them on a deep level. She knows what other people are feeling and their desires, and her primary goal is to fulfill their needs and desires.

However, as we will explore, the unskilled or unconscious Mother tends to experience burnout, fatigue, overwhelm, and exhaustion. This is because she often forgets to ask for help and sets no boundaries. Thus, it is crucial to understand the needs of the Mother and practice self-care to prevent burnout.

We will now delve deeper into the power of the Mother archetype, and learn how to embody her strengths while avoiding the pitfalls.

BECOMING THE MOTHER

Our mothers are our first teachers in the art of nurturing and taking care of others. Whether present in our lives or not, we learn from their example and the way they cared for us and others. This is both good and bad news, depending on your circumstances. You may end up following in your mother's footsteps or you may resist becoming like her. In either case, we are all shaped by our mother's energy.

Our mothers' impact on us runs deep, often subconsciously affecting our decisions, actions, and emotions. Even if we do not realize it, we may be carrying on their traditions, habits, and ways of being. This is the power of the Mother archetype, which can both empower and restrict us.

To fully embody the power of the Mother, we must first recognize and understand the impact our own mother had on us. This can be a challenging and emotional process, but it is a crucial step in breaking free from the limitations of the past and opening up to new possibilities.

By examining the role of the Mother in our lives and understanding how we relate to this archetype, we can start to make conscious choices about who we want to be and how we want to show up in the world. We can let go of old patterns and embrace new ways of being, fully embracing the power of the Feminine.

So, whether you're following in your mother's footsteps or breaking free from them, the Mother archetype remains a powerful force in your life. It is up to you to choose how you will embody this energy and shape your own path.

As you start to object, allow me to explain. Even if your intention is to become the complete opposite of your mother, your every thought and action is rooted in a subconscious effort to avoid turning into her. You may have heard the phrase "what you resist, persists." In fact, you may even make choices simply to ensure that you are nothing like her. Nevertheless, by doing so, you remain under her control. Your behavior and decisions are governed by what you observed or knew about your mother, and you are still being influenced by the same thoughts and beliefs that you are trying to resist. This may not be the news you were hoping for, but fear not, there is a way to break free from this pattern.

Personally, I resisted my mother's energy, her way of being, and her role as a mother. My mother worked full-time just like my dad. That is where the similarity ended. My mother was proud to work. Her own mother, after all, was not allowed to work even though she had great ambitions of becoming a doctor. While my mother was the first generation of women who could be in the workplace and have their own career, equal rights and opportunity, just like men, she also maintained the traditional mother role. While both my parents worked, when dad came home, his day was over. When mom came home, she strapped on her apron for her second full time job. As soon as she came home, she did all the cooking, the cleaning, the dishes, the laundry, she took care of the kids, sewed our clothes, fed the animals and prepared for the next day of work. It feels exhausting just to write this. All while my dad sat in front of the TV, read the newspaper, or did whatever he wanted to unwind from a long day at work.

As a young girl, I witnessed this dynamic that left me disenchanted with traditional gender roles. My mother, a trailblazing first-generation career woman, worked just as hard as my father, yet was still expected to shoulder the lion's share of domestic responsibilities. I had no appreciation for my mom and her role as a woman because there didn't seem to be any reward in it, just a whole lot of extra work. And that didn't sound fun to me. Growing up as my father's daughter, I wanted to be just like my dad. I had no respect for what I perceived as the feminine role. I longed to break free from the domestic sphere, forge my own path, and build my career. The thought of being chained to the kitchen or to my children or working myself to death with no reward seemed exhausting, stifling and unfulfilling.

As an adult, I made a conscious decision to reject the traditional feminine role that I saw growing up. When I got married, I refused to clean or cook, equating nurturing with self-sacrifice. I was determined not to become the kind of mother who was taken advantage of and treated like a maid. However, my resistance to anything resembling my mother's role was so strong that I threw out anything remotely feminine and fought constantly with my spouse over household chores. I failed to realize that in rejecting this role, I was denying a part of myself and the value of the work my mother had done.

REJECTING THE FEMININE

I missed out on the true essence of being a woman. Raised to see my mother as a servant to everyone's needs, I developed a deep aversion to anything remotely feminine. Instead, I adopted a masculine energy, abandoning any feminine qualities I possessed in my pursuit of success and financial security. I saw it as a choice between the two: all or nothing. In my eyes, success equated to competing with men, living in a man's world, and denying my femininity. I wanted to be a mini version of my father and gain control and credit for my work. But in doing so, I overlooked the incredible work my mother did, the sacrifices she made, and what she stood for.

With a laser focus on success, I put my head down, worked long hours, and never asked for help. I aimed to be the best man in the room, tackling every challenge head-on and never giving myself permission to embrace my feminine side. I was so determined to prove myself that I became drained, overworked, and exhausted. I grew tired of the constant competition and never allowed myself to receive help.

SEWING DREAMS AND NURTURING SOULS

My mother was a loving, giving mother. I now realize that I often took my mother for granted. She was always there for my brother and me, a constant source of love and comfort. There were so many moments of warmth and joy that I didn't fully appreciate at the time. Like the rainy Saturday mornings when she would make us hot chocolate. I can still feel the warmth of the mug in my hands and taste the sweetness of the marshmallows as we sat on the porch in her oversized fluffy robes, taking extra care to fold it under our feet as we sat watching the rain fall. It was a simple moment, but one that I now cherish.

Or the times when she would playfully tickle me, denying my pleas to go outside in our not-so-safe neighborhood. "I wanna play outside," I would beg, and she would tickle me and sing, "No playing outside." We would go back and forth like that, our duet of denial and laughter echoing through the house. I continued to ask, forgetting my initial plea, but reveling in her love and attention. I can now appreciate her clever way of saying no while still making me feel loved and attended to.

Growing up, I loved clothes. I wanted to be a model and designer. What girl didn't? I would draw beautiful clothes, inspired by runway fashion and clothes I would see on the red carpet. As I'm writing this, tears are flowing because my mom would actually create the designs I drew. She spent hours into the night, night after night, sewing, even after her long day of work and her chores were complete.

Most of the dresses came out beautiful, exactly or even better than I had envisioned. Some were not quite as I pictured in my mind. My tears come from the gratitude I now have for her love and gift as well as for her patience. They also flow for the shame I now feel for not appreciating her efforts. There were times, and it's difficult to write this, where I acted like a spoiled brat, getting upset at her for making something too long or not having the right cut. She never balked, she just went back to fixing the outfit according to my specifications.

My house was the home everyone gathered for the holidays. We would have dozens of people over. Anyone and everyone who didn't have a place to go would be invited to come over. My mom would work for days to prepare delectable desserts, incredible savory dishes and homemade breads. She would move furniture around to assure everyone had a place for a sit down meal and set the table beautifully with handpicked flowers from her garden and her best china. At one point, we may have had over 30 people and somehow, she found a place for everyone at the table in our small, modest home.

I failed to honor my mother for the love and care she gifted our family and all those around her. I was blind to the beautiful giving nature she carried into every interaction with others. I took for granted the beautiful meals she prepared, the loving haven she created in our home and the welcoming environment she created for guests. I didn't respect the part of her that was loving and in tune with people she cared about and I failed to recognize that she was a loving and devoted mother.

She died young, and even to this day, whenever I meet someone who had the privilege of knowing her, they inevitably speak of her in glowing terms. They comment on the effortless grace with which she opened up her home to others, the undeniable talent she had for cooking up a storm, and the way she made each and every person feel truly seen and valued in her presence.

The gift that my mother, and all mothers, bring to those around them is beautiful. When they create a comfortable and welcoming home or prepare a delicious meal to nourish those they love, or when they selflessly care for those around them, those are gifts that should be cherished in all women.

HEALING THE MOTHER RELATIONSHIP

Healing our relationship with our own mother will allow us to clear out any negative programming and limiting decisions we have made around being a woman, being a mother, and owning or denying the feminine part of ourselves. Whether or not you are or will ever be a mother, this feminine archetype is essential in opening up to the fullness of your expression as a woman and to be able to give and receive help, resources, abundance, love, and health in your life. Once healed, you can step into your powerful Mothering energy, allowing you to heed the internal feminine call to connect and contribute to the world while maintaining your boundaries and internal locus of control.

In this healing visualization meditation, we will connect with our mother and examine what we have learned about being a mother, what beliefs, decisions, and energies we have picked up, and clear anything that disempowers us. We will also look at how we are either becoming our mother or resisting her and how that plays out in our lives. Are we able to nurture others? Do we feel resentful that we are not being nurtured? Can we receive the healing gift from other people?"

You can read this meditation, close your eyes and go through the process or listen to the meditation by visiting the following page: www.SweetSexyBadassQueen.com

MOTHER MEDITATION

Put your feet flat on the ground and take a couple of deep cleansing breaths. Send a spiritual hello to your body. If you need to adjust yourself in your chair go ahead and do that now. Take care that your body is comfortable and feels good. With your body open, no parts of your body crossed, what I would like you to do is go ahead and notice if you are still grounded. Do you have that grounding cord working for you; that rope attached to the base of your spine that extends all the way to the center of the planet. You might want to create a new one or just re-attach it. Give it a little tug, make sure you are comfortably sitting in your body right now. Make sure your mind is not going out somewhere trying to heal, fix, or take care of anything or anyone outside of you. If it is, simply and gently bring your attention back to your body. Be here in the Now, fully present in your body. This is the time for you.

What I would like you to do is about three feet behind you and off to your right, create in your mind's eye a platform. Imagine seeing a 3X3 platform made of whatever material you choose, wood, marble or carpet. Put a grounding cord on that platform.

Say hello to your own birth mother and ask your mother to go ahead and stand on that platform. If someone else raised you, you can do this again with her but first, I invite you to work with the mother that gave you the body. Whether or not she is alive in a physical body, she can still come and stand on that platform. Then you can go ahead and have her first step a little bit closer, about one foot behind you, and just notice what happens to you. Notice what happens to your body as she comes closer.

Are you excited that she's here with you or is there a little bit of resistance to her? Is your body contracting or do you feel expansion? Are you breathing? Bring her closer so she is directly to your right. Say hello to her and notice how it feels when she is that close to you. Notice what lights up in you. You may feel a tingling sensation, you may feel light or you may feel a heaviness somewhere in your body or around the edges of your body. What memories, thoughts, sensations, images or feelings come to mind? What beliefs does she light up in you? Without resisting any of these thoughts, or feelings that come up, just be present with them. Don't fight them, don't try to change them, just notice. The loving presence you can give yourself while this comes up allows you to lovingly release any negative charge.

Imagine beautiful, neutral purple dust being tossed in your space and imagine this purple dust sticking to any place in your body or your aura, the electromagnetic field around your body, where you feel energy light up. These are places where you have a match with your mother, where you have energy that is just like hers. Maybe how she speaks, how she lives her life or how she treats other people. Perhaps it's how she takes care of herself or how she doesn't take care of herself, how she gives to others or how she doesn't give to others. Do you have a match with her role as a mother, did she take on that role voluntarily or was it forced upon her? Notice the purple dust sticking to any place in your body or the space around your body where you are "just like your mother". Notice those places light up with the purple dust. As it sticks, you'll notice purple dots sticking to your body and your aura, to pictures where you have similar beliefs and made similar decisions. This can be conscious or you can trust your unconscious to find and stick to any of your matches. The beauty of this work is you don't have to consciously see it for it to work.

Imagine creating a rose out in front of you and take that rose with your hand and begin to move it through your space. Imagine that rose turning into a vacuum rose picking up all those purple dots. Allow it to pick up all the pictures, all those matches around your body and around your aura, the space just outside of your body. Watch it easily and effortlessly suck up all the purple dots, just like a vacuum. When all those purple dots have gone into that rose, take that rose and put it out about four feet in front of you and put a little firecracker under that rose. Blow that rose up, turning it into pure energy, and observe as the rose completely disintegrates. Notice that there is nothing left of that rose.

Now imagine some purple dust being tossed into your space and this time it sticks to any place in your body and your aura where you are in resistance to your mother and what she stands for. Maybe you have a match but you've consciously or even unconsciously decided not to be anything like her. The match may still be there even if you denounced something about her and decided not to repeat her pattern. These are places where you resist her beliefs, her decisions, how she acted and how she interacted. These are places where you decided to make sure you are going to do the polar opposite of what she did and the choices she made. You decided to never do what you saw her do, or what she told you to do, or what her role was as a woman or as a mother. This may be conscious or unconscious. Any place where you are in resistance, where you refuse to be "just like her". Notice how many purple dots there are in your space and notice where they collect. Create another rose and take that rose and turn it into a vacuum. Watch it suck up all those dots, all those purple points around you. Run that through your body and through your aura. When all those purple dots are gone, go ahead and take that rose out in front of your body, in front of your aura, about 3-4 feet, and again put a little firecracker under there and blow up that rose.

Notice if you can say hello to your mother a little easier now. Is it easier to have her so close to you? Can you now see her as a separate person, a separate woman, independent of you and who you are? Can you separate your identity from her identity? Just notice if you are able to recognize, accept, or say hello to your own ability to be a mother, whether or not you have children. We are all caretakers of our bodies, our aura, our neighborhoods, our communities and our planet. Notice if you are able to say hello to your own ability to be a mother, to nurture yourself and others, to be in touch with the Mother Feminine type within you.

You can take a minute to forgive and thank your mother, and then have her step back about three feet behind you, back onto that platform. Set an intention that she is getting her own clearing and her own healing from divinity. Allow her to go back to where she belongs, out of your space. Now go ahead and create a big golden sun above your head. Start to call back all your energy into that golden sun. Watch that sun get big and bright, filling up completely with your beautiful essence. When it's all filled up, start to bring that golden light into your body, into your aura, from the top of your head all the way down to the tips of your toes. Every place where you released energy, where you let go of old programs, old beliefs, old limiting decisions, old attachments, fill in that space with your golden light. And when you are all filled up, take a deep breath, come on out, open your eyes, stand up, move around and stretch your body.

YOUR JOURNAL

Take a few minutes to journal about what you experienced, any ah-ha's you had. What you learned and what you let go of during this process?

Now that you have cleared any resistance to opening up to your Inner Mother, let's explore a little more about this beautiful Feminine energy.

Four

THE INNER MOTHER

"The most important thing a mother can do for her children is to love herself because through her love for herself, she teaches them to love themselves. And when they love themselves, they become the kind of person who can change the world."

STEPPING INTO THE INNER MOTHER

The Mother is all about making people comfortable, anticipating their needs, giving and receiving. The mother in me shares food at random times at work and always when I hold a meeting as a way of nurturing my staff. The mother in me loves to create beautiful parties. As I am writing this, I am preparing a wonderful Easter brunch, complete with gorgeous flowers, carefully selected music, perfect decorations, and delicious food. The mother in me makes sure my son is happy and that all his needs are met to help him feel loved and taken care of.

One thing to note is that although the part of giving is from the Feminine Mother, the “doing” part of giving is where the CEO steps in and makes it happen.

But being a mother isn't just about giving. It's also about receiving. An unbalanced mother is someone who never learned to say "no" or set boundaries. She gives and gives until she's depleted, forgetting her own needs in the process. In extreme cases, she may become a martyr, sacrificing everything for the sake of others. This is why a woman may simply decide to stop giving out of resentment, rather than creating balance in her life. The Mother archetype is a powerful force for giving and receiving, but she needs the support of the other archetypes to truly thrive.

To truly give and receive in balance, a mother must learn to set boundaries and recognize her own needs. That's where the CEO comes in. This archetype helps her to put her foot down and say "no" when necessary, ensuring that she doesn't become taken advantage of or feel obligated to give more than she can. And while the Mother knows how to say "yes" with love and compassion, the CEO balances that with practicality and self-care.

The Playmate, on the other hand, helps the Mother get in touch with her desires and needs. This archetype encourages her to take time for herself and do things that bring her joy and fulfillment. And finally, the High Priestess helps the Mother to give and receive in a way that is truly meaningful and beneficial for all involved. She ensures that the Mother is giving from a place of authenticity and that her giving is truly making a difference.

THE LINE BETWEEN MOTHERING AND SMOTHERING

Let's talk about mothering. Everyone loves a woman who is loving, nurturing, and attentive. But there's a fine line between being caring and being smothering. You know the type: the woman who constantly asks if you're okay, always jumping in to rescue those she loves, saving the day, or fixing problems without allowing others to take responsibility for their own lives. She means well, of course, but her actions can become suffocating, annoying, and even a turnoff for men. After all, men want a woman who is nurturing, but they also want to maintain their manhood and independence. If a woman treats a man like a child, he will start to lose attraction for her. It's simple - who wants to have sex with their mother?

A balanced mother knows when to give and when to step back. Hovering is never attractive and men in particular do not like to be mothered. Jumping in and offering unsolicited help or advice in a relationship is sending a message that you do not trust your man to take care of business. While a mother loves to give and help, a balanced mother knows the line between giving and creating a co-dependent relationship.

When a mother becomes overly involved in her children's lives, constantly swooping in to solve their problems and shield them from life's challenges, she robs them of the opportunity to learn and grow on their own. In effect, she creates a co-dependent relationship in which the child is unable to function independently and lacks the resilience needed to navigate life's ups and downs. She'll then wonder why her child is still sleeping in her basement, eating her food and "in-between" jobs at the age of 35.

Children need to learn to take risks and experience failure without being constantly rescued. Men need to be able to make decisions and be given the space to be the provider and decision maker. Often smothering comes from insecurity, a desire to be valued and loved for what she can give. The desire to make someone dependent on you can be a misguided attempt to secure affection and attention. Women often have a deep seated fear of abandonment and will deal with it in unconstructive ways. If this resonates with you, take heart. The healing process starts with getting in touch with your Inner High Priestess. This archetype can help you to identify and heal the wounds that are driving your fear of abandonment and your need to be needed. With her guidance, you can learn to let go of the past and embrace a future filled with love, security, and independence.

DANGERS OF CARING FOR OTHERS

The Mother is the giver of life. She literally delivers human life and also gives birth to new ideas. She nurtures people, thoughts and ideas and provides nourishment of the body, mind and soul. She gives unconditionally and is a fountain of love. There is no stopping the amount of love that she can give, when left to her own devices, that is.

She gives her all to her children, even when they test her patience, push her buttons, and test the limits. She doesn't give up on them, even when they make bad choices, like falling behind in school or experimenting with harmful substances. She is a beacon of hope, a pillar of strength, and a source of comfort in their darkest hours. She is the embodiment of selflessness and devotion, and her unwavering love is a constant reminder of the beauty of motherhood. She is patient and kind; she is devoted, caring, and unselfish.

When we speak of being a protector and nurturer of life, we often think of children. However, this quality extends beyond them to include those around her; spouse, family, friends, co-workers, and even strangers. This aspect of the Feminine is often drawn to help children around the world or being involved in a charity. She can take on community and global problems and serve as a volunteer, advocate, leader or voice for the people. With a motherly quality, she has the capacity to care for everyone she encounters.

When taking care of so many people and mothering everybody, one of the problems she can face is getting out of sync with herself resulting in feeling deprived and resentful, as she has a finite amount of energy to give. The more she gives to others without refueling herself, the more disconnected she can become from herself. This can lead the Mother toward co-dependence, taking on more responsibility for others' happiness and well-being than they do themselves.

BREAKING THE CHAINS OF MARTYRDOM

A martyr is someone who unnecessarily sacrifices themselves for others, while ignoring their own needs. Sound like anyone you know? As we've mentioned many times, the Mother is the part of a woman that can connect with others. She knows what they think, need, and feel, often before they do. The Mother says 'yes' to her kids, friends, family, and job. She's so in tune with those around her that she can anticipate their feelings and desires, understanding them on a deep level and providing for them. Can you see how beautiful this is? Can you also see how dangerous this can be?

The Mother can easily lose herself in others. It is the mother that doesn't know who she is when the children are gone. So many women give their whole lives to their children, and when they leave the nest, they often feel empty and alone. A woman can spend her entire marriage trying to make her husband happy, doing everything for him and making him comfortable, and when he unexpectedly leaves, she is left broken, empty, and has lost all sense of herself. She spent so much of her life tuning into what others need that when she is finally left on her own, she can't even articulate what she desires, what makes her happy and what she needs. She doesn't know who she is and has lost her sense of separateness. She spent so much of her energy sacrificing for others, ignoring her needs, that after some time, she no longer is in touch with her own needs.

The Mother will require all her Feminine Types to keep her feeling beautiful, powerful and at peace with herself. She requires the High Priestess to keep her in touch with her heart, her higher self and her inner knowing that will remind her who she is and prevent her from getting lost in everyone else's needs. The Playmate reminds her to have fun, gets her in touch with daily self care and pleasure and the CEO keeps score, helps her set boundaries when she has given too much and prevents her from feeling empty and depleted. The CEO will assist her in regaining the balance and saying NO when necessary.

Five

BREAKING THE BINDS

"When we break the cycle of over-giving, we create space for ourselves to receive the love and care we deserve, and in turn, we are better able to give from a place of abundance rather than depletion."

OVER GIVING

We all have people who depend on us. For some, it's their children, for others, it could be employees or extended family members. The Mother can suffer from over-giving with any of these groups without requiring them to step up and give back. This means things like chores, participating in the responsibilities around the home, and picking up the slack at work. This can be especially true in the workplace, where a woman's maternal instincts can lead her to take on more than her fair share of work. She stays late to cover for others, says yes to every request, and sacrifices her own projects for the good of the team.

Although from a work ethic point of view, this can be admirable, it needs to be under the watchful eye of your internal CEO so that you don't sacrifice to the point of burn out. Practice making requests and make the request in a nonjudgmental non-overly motherly manner. Make the request without nagging and in a non-condescending manner. Be willing to ask for support, share the workload and accept the help. You don't have to do it all yourself.

CO-DEPENDENT NO MORE

In order to save herself from giving too much, the Mother requires the High Priestess and the CEO by her side. The High Priestess connects her with universal love while the CEO will tell her when enough is enough. Connecting with the higher part of you, healing any past trauma or attachment to needing to be the savior or needing to be loved is required. Gaining higher ground where you acknowledge that everyone has their own answers and path in life, and that it's not up to you to "save" them, is the gift of the High Priestess. While the High Priestess helps you stay present to any discomfort or bubbling up feeling of resentment or being taken advantage of, the CEO can step in and put her foot down. The CEO can unapologetically pull away from a dysfunctional relationship or dynamic and simply say "No".

BREAKING THE CYCLE OF OVERWORKING

The unskilled mother often forgets to ask for help. She needs to learn how to ask for help and to do it without feeling guilty. There's such a sense of duty in the mother that she feels like she has to take care of everybody. When she is tired and exhausted, what women normally do is sit back and start to feel resentful. We start to get angry. She asks, why am I doing all this? Why can't somebody else do the dishes or take out the trash or earn the money. Why doesn't anybody help me? Yet we don't seek help, or try anything different until we get resentful and angry.

She may blow up at her kids, demand more help from her husband, or shut down altogether. She might step back for a little bit, get angry, or lash out. However, this never lasts and doesn't produce any real help. Eventually, the mother instinct kicks in. The Mother is very forgiving. Because the unbalanced Mother doesn't know another way, once she gets over those emotions, she sucks it up and goes back to work. Yet, she doesn't really get over it. She stuffs it in, sucks it up, and continues to do the same thing until she runs into the next level of exhaustion, creates the next level of resentment and anger, and the cycle continues.

Women are good at doing their jobs. We're great at being mothers, wives, business owners, and taking care of everyone else. This is because women are capable, but we forget that we also need to lean back and be taken care of. We need to learn to ask for help.

Hopefully I've convinced you to ask for help. Now, what does that look like? We are going to need the help of the other Feminine types in order to ask for help in the most powerful, fun and effective manner. I'll touch on them here and go into them in detail in the respective sections.

When we ask for help from any man, a spouse or significant other, a co-worker, even a child, we do so directly, unapologetically and respectfully. I have a 25 year old son and I really had to learn this at a young age because even though I was his mother, I had to make sure I wasn't emasculating him and taking away his manhood. There are powerful words that we use that will shut a man down and there are powerful words we can use that will allow him to rise up and be our hero. We need heroes in our lives. That is what will keep us going and increase our ability to give. We need someone that will take care of us, someone that will support us and do the heavy lifting for us. And most people are happy to be of service when asked the right way.

ASKING FOR HELP

What does asking for help actually look like? For starters, it's not about treating someone like a child or barking orders at them. It's not nagging or resorting to angry demands when things don't go as planned. I can remember when my son was younger, and how I used to get so frustrated with the trash piling up - one of the few chores he had - that I would end up going off on a rant. "Why didn't you take out the trash? You always leave it, and it just piles up. I'm sick and tired of it," I would say. Looking back, I can see how I fell into the trap of berating him, which didn't do anything for his confidence and actually made him resist my plea.

The CEO makes the request powerfully and confidently, the High Priestess respects herself enough to know she deserves it and is respectful of the man in question and the Playmate asks in a fun, playful way, taking all the seriousness and drudgery out of the question.

When making a request of a man, it is important to use the words "will you" rather than "can you". When you ask "can you take out the trash" or "can you pick up milk from the store", a man is thrown off and feels insulted. To a man, "can you" questions his ability. His internal response is, of course I can, of course I am capable, what kind of question is that. When you ask "will you take out the trash", you come from a confident place and this asserts your self-authority? Confidence is sexy. Confidence is powerful. We want to be confident when we are making a request and you want to be confident enough to give the man a choice.

When you ask “will you”, he will either say yes or no. Part of asking is being prepared for his answer, no matter what it is. Being prepared for him to say no, and then be willing to accept that or have another consequence or have an alternative request is power. Of course, the CEO knows that if a man repeatedly denies your request, you take that as information and you respond accordingly.

For women, “can you” and “will you” are interchangeable. In fact, using “can you” is much more respectful for a woman. It is a gentle request. For a man, it is much different. I didn't really get the difference until someone said just imagine being proposed to by a man. He brings you flowers. He takes you on a beautiful date. You are out on the balcony of a beautiful restaurant on the ocean and the sun is setting. You just finished a delectable dessert and he gets down on one knee, opens up a box with a diamond ring and says, “Can you marry me”?

If you are like most women, your excitement just deflated. If you are like me, this just rubbed you the wrong way. What do you mean, “Can I marry you”? “Do you want me to marry you or not”? When he asks, “Will you marry me”, there is a profound shift in the vibration of that request. This question instills confidence in you, it affirms that he has made a choice and has conviction over that choice. It inspires the woman to join him in his conviction. That is how important it is for men to hear “will you”.

So when you make a request, “will you pick up the groceries for me, will you take out the trash, will you put gas in my car” you are confidently making a request honoring yourself as the recipient and honoring the man. You are giving him a choice, not acting like his mother and not treating him like a child.

The flip side of this is accepting assistance being offered. One of the things that I see happen so often is that men will try to assist you or help you and because we are very capable, strong, powerful, independent women, we forget to allow men to take care of us. I can't tell you how many times a man has offered to carry a bag for me. And I said, oh no, no, thank you, I've got it. Why do I say that? Because I don't want to put him through the trouble. I don't want to inconvenience him. I know this bag is heavy and I don't want to make him work extra hard.

The thought of that now is a joke to me. He is stronger than you, he is supposed to flex his muscles. That is what they love to do, that is their way of feeling needed, useful and powerful. Just like the Mother loves to gift, the man loves to care for and protect in slightly different ways. Helping you and being your hero actually makes him feel more like a man, especially when he is appreciated for what he does. When you refuse to allow a man to let you go through a doorway first and you insist on walking behind him, you are making him question his inherent protective and chivalrous ways. When a man wants to put his coat on you because you are cold or shivering, or it is a windy day and you are outdoors and you say, no thank you, you have just crushed his heart and his attempt to be your hero at that moment.

From now on, resolve to take the damn coat. I'm talking to you like I talked to myself because there had been countless times where a man has tried to give me his jacket and all I thought was "I don't want you to be cold, I don't want you to shiver, if you give me your jacket, you are only going to have a shirt. That's okay, I will sacrifice. I will sit here freezing and shivering". That is acting like his mother and I tell you ladies, no man is attracted to his mother. Stop acting like his mother. I can kick myself for the amount of times I've done that in my life. Now when a man offers me his jacket, I tell myself, Trez, take the damn coat, let him be your hero. And of course, be delighted in his quest to protect you. Share your appreciation by saying thank you, showing delight in your smile or physically touching or hugging him.

I notice a different response from men when I allow them to be my hero. They start stepping up in other ways, because for them, it is refreshing finding a woman who truly knows how to receive and is gracious when receiving. These days, men crave the appreciation they get from being your hero. You have a chance to gift him that beautiful gift he is so longing for. I've had plenty of men tell me it is so refreshing to be with a woman who is so gracious and grateful for the little things he does for me.

There are other times when you can gently invite a man to step up in little ways like opening doors. I will even slow down to allow a man to open doors for me. There was one man I went out on a date with and we were holding hands walking to the car after dinner. He let go of my hand and was about to walk around to his side of the car. It caught me off guard for a second because I was used to men opening the door for me.

There is a simple way to invite the man to step up. We need to understand that when men are not stepping up, when men are not doing the chivalrous things, when men are not taking care of you the way you deserve to be taken care of, the way you would take care of other people, it is simply because they have been trained out of it.

If you were with an elderly parent or child, you would open the door for them. When a man doesn't do it, it is not because he doesn't care about you. It is not because he doesn't love you. It is not because he is being rude or obnoxious or lazy. It is usually because he either has not been trained or he has tried and was berated by women one too many times, who have reminded him that she doesn't need him, and that she can do this herself.

I grabbed him by the hand, and I pulled him close. I gave him a little kiss and I said, "Aren't you gonna open the door for me?" in my sexy girl voice. He immediately responded, oh yeah. He opened the door and I got in the car and I made sure to thank him with a little smile that says, I just so appreciate you, you're such a wonderful man. He never failed to open the door for me again and I always said thank you and showed him some love.

We need to show our appreciation to men, show our devotion and shower them with physical affection when they do things for us. The Playmate is great at this. Appreciation makes the man step up and want to give more to you. One of the reasons that we as women are exhausted is that we are doing the work for the men in our lives. Even in the workforce, we are doing the work for the men that we work with. We are not allowing them to step up because we feel that we need to prove ourselves. We are not allowing men in the workplace to be men and honor their instinct, which is to protect and to provide for us. When you do that, you will find yourself much more taken care of and less exhausted.

Six

SELF WORTH

"A woman's greatest asset is her beauty - and it begins with knowing and valuing her worth."

THE BEAST AND THE BEAUTY

Most of us graduated from being the fair maiden, awaiting rescue by Prince Charming on a white horse, to being the rescuer in Beauty and the Beast. In this tale, the dreadful Beast is transformed by the power of the beautiful and loving Beauty, who saw in the monster behind his anger and egocentric, narcissistic and crass behavior, only beauty. As he was quickly losing life, she declared her undying unconditional love for him and the spell was broken. He magically turned into a handsome prince and they "lived happily ever after".

For many women, this is the beginning of their demise. They find a man who is a hot mess but has great potential. These women are smart and savvy enough to see his flaws, yet they feel they can transform him into their knight in shining armor through the power of their unconditional love and affection. The loving Mother steps in. She finds the man she can fix and goes about loving and taking care of him. She works at proving to him how lovable he is. She coaches him, mothers him, takes care of his needs, supports him in building "his dreams" and makes excuses for his anger, flakiness, unfaithfulness or absence.

Meanwhile, the beast never changes, after-all, a beast is just a beast. He is happy to take her money and to allow her to take care of his laundry, children and run around to try to make him comfortable. He is happy to continue to have a home to come home to when he screws up, cheats on her, gets caught in his lies, allows his anger to tear her spirit apart and take every last bit of self respect she has for herself. And he is happy to get his ego boosted undeservingly while he takes advantage of her unconditional love, uses her up until she is left with nothing and turns her into someone she no longer recognizes.

When a woman finds herself in a relationship like this, she needs to step back and assess the part she plays. If you've come out of one, congratulations. Learn the warning signs and vow to love yourself more than you could sacrifice for others.

Too often, a woman becomes so weighed down by the darkness and problems of the man in front of her that she loses sight of herself. You hear women go on and on about her man's indiscriminate ways followed by a piteous "but I love him". You may ask why would a strong loving woman fall for this trap and get caught up in the downward spiral of getting ripped apart, used up and spit out. I've worked with many women who beat themselves up after having had such an experience wondering how they could have been so weak, so dumb, so naïve.

On the contrary, I have found that it is the strong woman, the one who initially has great regard for herself and loads of love to give, that falls into this trap. She feels she has enough love for the both of them and can sustain the relationship with her strength, love and willpower. It's not her weakness that draws her to him but her strength. Yet it is her inexperience that keeps her there. She doesn't know that it will not end well. What actually happens over time is she loses love for herself. In fact, she loses herself altogether. The truth is, no man can be saved. Yes, a woman can provide a loving devoted space for a man to become the best man he can be but she has to recognize the difference between a mutually beneficial loving relationship and falling into the trap of a narcissist who only cares about himself.

A woman who finds herself in this space can first recognize that she may be dancing too much on the loving and giving space. She needs to bring in her CEO that can put a stake in the ground and declare that she is not going to enable any man, woman or child for that matter to live in a dependent, helpless place. She will no longer give in to all requests and demands placed on her. She will no longer take their plea for help as a prompt for her to step up and take responsibility to make up for their lack. Her inner CEO says no thank you. I will not partake in this co-dependent, dysfunctional relationship and I will not allow you to deplete me of my precious energy. I will not walk on egg shells so that you don't get upset, I will not hide your bottles after a drunken night, and I will not cover up your mess. I will not take responsibility for your debauched choices and I will not allow you to quietly and insidiously put me down as an attempt to make yourself feel superior or crush and take away my spirit.

I NEED A HERO

Which leads us to another epidemic where we are not only hurting ourselves, but we are hurting our men. Women are hurting men and their manhood because we have been guilty of making sure that they know we don't need them. I was taught not to depend on men. I believe this was an important step for me and other women gaining independence from the dominant masculine control. This was crucial to a woman's ability to stand up for herself and leave abusive or oppressive conditions. This allowed a woman to chart her own course in life and go after her goals and ambitions. Women were no longer trapped, knowing she could take care of herself. This has allowed her to walk away from bad marriages and other harmful situations. However, in an effort to prove her independence, many women have gone to the extreme, berating men for being gentlemen and wanting to take care of or provide for her. I have heard countless stories of men being attacked for opening up doors for women, to the point where they are either hesitant or they flat out no longer try to be chivalrous in order to protect their ego. I also know women, myself included, who at one point refused to allow a man to pick up the tab for fear of owing him anything. We sadly drove the chivalry out of the man.

The essence of masculine energy is to provide for, to take care of, to protect and to be needed. When we deny men that opportunity to take care of us, to protect us, we are denying their manhood as well. Not only are we denying their manhood, we are making them wrong for stepping into their masculinity. In addition, we are becoming more masculine and hurting our own lives. My advice, let the man be the man, let him take care of you, protect you and revel in his care. Allow yourself to receive. And don't worry, your CEO will make sure you don't become too dependent on him or his care. She will always be there to make sure you have choices. You can leave if you need to, pay your own bills if you have to and take up the reins when required.

BONDING

The Mother is a pro at bonding. Bonding is one of the most basic human drives. Children are first bonded to their mothers and then the bond shifts to the people around them. The opposite of bonding is self-sufficiency. One of the things that hurt women over the last 50 years is this idea that we need to be self sufficient, that we need to take care of ourselves, and that we shouldn't need anybody. We learned that needing others is a sign of weakness. Having to do it all alone is a huge lie and is one of the sad casualties of the whole feminist and equal rights era.

Women swung to the opposite side of the pendulum where instead of being so dependent on the men in their lives, they wanted to be completely independent of other people. They rebuffed asking men for help, they rejected their female tribe and they went into the jungle all alone, carrying nothing other than the clothes on their back.

The truth is that no man or woman is an island. Human beings are designed to be in groups, to cohabitate and to cooperate to achieve their goals. We cannot survive, we cannot function, we cannot create, we cannot continue to do what we are doing without having bonds with other people. A woman has trouble knowing herself without connecting with others, without asking for help, without allowing people to support her and to provide for her while she moves forward in her life. She also knows herself through giving to others. Hillary Clinton wrote "It takes a village to raise a child". The idea of the village has been in our history, throughout the ages. This is how our species has survived existence for so long. No person can create big shifts on their own. We women in particular, require the bonds of the people around us to lift us up, to support us, to provide for our needs, in not only surviving, but in thriving. We require assistance in filling our buckets and achieving our dreams. This interdependence allows you as a woman to continue to hold space for others to step into their greatness and for them to hold space for you.

Women, even as recent as the last generation, bonded with other women in order to get support, nourishment and love from each other. It was required so that women can continue to give at a level that is needed in our society. Women were taking care of their children, their spouses, their family and when they needed to be nourished, when they needed to be nurtured, they went to their female tribe. They received a boost of energy, support, love, and mothering from their female tribe. In contrast, women today are so busy taking care of others, we forget that we also need to be mothered. Today, women are programmed to continue to give, yet, because they have dejected the tribe, have no real way of refueling. For those who are married or in a relationship, the expectation then turns to the men in their lives, looking to them for constant nurturing which strips them of their own masculinity. Men get blamed for "not being there" for their women in the way only a woman can, and are confused about their own role in a relationship. Women are increasingly isolated and feeling the need to fend for themselves, not knowing any other options.

The drive to be self-sufficient, to take care of themselves, to figure life out alone, is depleting women. Thinking we need to man up, take the bull by the horns, be successful and do it on our own is really one of the major reasons why women are running off fumes right now. This is why we are getting exhausted, this is why we are getting depressed, this is why we are not getting taken care of and this is why we are getting sick.

The remedy, surround yourself with a loving supportive tribe of women. Find positive, like minded women you trust to connect with. Decide to give to each other, spend time talking, having fun and participating in self care activities together. Connect regularly and allow yourself to be vulnerable. Share your thoughts, share your feelings and practice listening to each other. Ask for help and graciously receive it. When you are called to, offer your own assistance in specific meaningful ways.

LEARN THE ART OF CONVERSATION

Learn the art of conversation. . . please. My son and I were having dinner at a restaurant and were interrupted by a loud woman having a conversation with a young man whom she obviously barely knew. She began by sharing how open she and her boyfriend were and explained in detail, that she had many, many, many friends who were guys. She continued to stress this point throughout her conversation. In case he didn't understand or get it the first time, she continued explaining that most of her friends were guys and that she had many, many friends who were male. He was obviously unimpressed. She went on to describe that her boyfriend says it's okay for her to meet these men for lunch or coffee, that it was no big deal. I'm not sure if he knew whether he was going on a date or taking a girl out for a free lunch but he quickly sank into his salad as soon as it was delivered. She took her first breath and excitedly said to him, "I bet you'll never guess", he didn't even try, "but I have a four year old daughter". I bet he would never have guessed. She went on to tell him about how she has her full time, exactly how she plans on raising her and that she is the reason she rarely gets to go out. I bet he was hoping she had to rush back home to relieve the babysitter. She wants her daughter to see the real world and then began to describe her version of the real world. I noticed when they first sat down, he made eye contact and was attempting to be pleasant but quickly realized, no matter what he did or said, she would continue to blabber on and on.

The entrée came and for a minute I thought my son and I were going to be able to enjoy our own conversation. She took a couple of bites and continued on about how she wanted to become a model, not a runway model, she clarified, but a model nonetheless. She would have to lose weight though and she was planning on doing that by exercising and eating healthy. She was already eating fairly healthy though and she didn't want to bulk up but would somehow workout enough to be a model. At this point, he just stared at each bite of food as it was entering his mouth, probably saying a silent prayer for her to please shut up.

Have you ever met someone who made you feel completely comfortable in their presence? They were the complete opposite of this woman. They asked you about your day and you felt they really cared about your answer. The Mother is a great listener. She is an expert at making people feel comfortable and feel important. And it often starts with the first hello. She is able to connect with others and allow them space to feel heard, to feel seen and to be loved and respected for who they are. While the CEO can have powerful conversations that get to the point, and the Playmate can participate in playful banter or engaging storytelling to lighten the mood and make people feel validated, the Mother has heart to heart conversations that make people feel seen.

Say hello, ask a person something about themselves and be curious. Find out what they love, what they are passionate about and why. Don't interrogate. Without turning it into 20 questions and an interview, give them the space to share who they are and let them guide the conversation in a free flow manner. The Mother loves learning about other people and genuinely loves to connect with others. She loves to learn about what makes them tick and who they are at their core. And she does this with 100% love and nonjudgement. This pure acceptance is palpable and undeniable.

Stepping into your inner Sweet Mother means having a genuine desire to give others space to be themselves. She does this by validating who they are and what they say. She accepts people 100%. Just like a mother unconditionally accepts and loves her child regardless of how they act at times, the Mother creates a beautiful space of acceptance, curiosity and genuine interest in others.

This in turn creates a safe space for others to open up, be vulnerable and share who they are inside.

THE CHALLENGE OF HAVING TEENAGERS

When my son was entering his teenage years, I knew I was heading toward a period of separation. He would be in his own world, turning to his peers instead of me and would lose touch with his mom. He was no longer interested in sharing his day with me and my series of questions would be met with one word answers or simple grunts. "How was your day?", I would ask. "Okay", he would say. "Anything exciting happen?" "Nah". Exhilarating conversations, I know. I eventually stumbled on a few tricks that would later assure he would open up to me.

One was the day I let him choose the music station to listen to in the car. I was always reluctant to listen to his music, not exactly my cup of tea, and oh, the cursing. Very offensive to me. One day I let him choose the station and sat quietly, albeit squirming in my seat with every foul connotation or word, but I was quiet. Something amazing happened. He began talking. Telling me stories of what was happening in his classroom, at school and on the football field. I realized the more I listened, the more he spoke. While every part of me wanted to ask more questions, to interject, to offer my brilliant advice or opinion, I kept my mouth shut. I listened, and he shared more. I even intentionally allowed space for the silence after he spoke. Silently counting to 30 seconds after he paused before I would say anything. Incredibly, often times, at around 20-25 seconds, he would chime in with more information. I was floored and deliriously happy. I had the intel into my son's life and I couldn't be happier.

When I am in a conversation with someone I care about, a client, a family member or a friend who is sharing something important, I often practice the 30 second rule. I listen to them talk without interrupting, and when they stop talking, I sit quietly in acknowledgement for at least 30 seconds without saying a word. What I find is, they will usually jump in with more to share. I found that this assists others in truly feeling heard and allows them to get to the heart of the matter. They feel seen by me, not judged, and they share more than just the surface of the issue.

The real test for me came when he shared stories or events that freaked me out. Things like being offered drugs, fights, confrontations, getting in trouble and girls. While every ounce of me wanted to react with horror, I kept my cool, acted like it was no big deal. “Some guys were passing around drugs in the locker room today”, he would calmly share. “Oh”, I would reply. “I just told them they were stupid and walked out” he continued. “Oh”, I would again reply. No reaction; good or bad. Of course I wanted to ask who, what, where, how often, have you ever taken drugs. But I knew sharing how much I was freaking out inside would quickly shut him down. I also knew if I started a lecture on the harmful long term effects of taking drugs, or that I should call the principal and let him know what was happening on his campus, he would also be wary of giving me any more information in the future. I simply acted like he just told me he ate a sandwich for lunch.

The result. . . he continued to open up and share. And what happened later surprised me even more, he started to ask for my advice. I knew this could easily be a trap and I had to tread lightly. I had to carefully craft my thoughts so as not to run with an onslaught of motherly wisdom. I definitely had much to share, but I held back. One sign of judgement and he would quickly shut down again. I would err on the side of asking more questions versus giving him advice. I am proud to say he kept me in the loop in his life which I feel kept him out of the at-risk group so many teens fall into when they feel they have to navigate the challenges of their teenage years all by themselves. In working with teens, I find they really need and desire adult wisdom. They just don't want to be lectured or told what to do. This is not to say kids should not have consequences or be given guidance on how to navigate through life, but what is important to understand is that the Mother can make a person feel seen and heard. When a person feels seen and heard, then they are more likely to respect you, look up to you and heed your wisdom and advice. "Seek first to understand and then to be understood" as Stephen Covey so eloquently shared. And by way, this has worked wonders in my romantic relationship. Whereas most women complain that their man doesn't open up to them, using this same practice has allowed the men around me to feel safe enough to open up and share themselves with me.

Seven

A MOTHER'S GIFT

"A mother's intuition is the strongest energy known to man. It knows no law, no pity, it dares all things and crushes down remorselessly all that stands in its path."

~ Agatha Christie ~

TUNING IN

To step into your Mother energy, start getting in tune with the people around you. As you are having a conversation with another person, focus on that person. Be present. Let go of any desire you have to jump in and offer your wisdom, ideas or insight. Don't try to change their mind, sway them in any direction, or throw in your two cents. Put yourself in their shoes. Truly listen to that person without reading into the conversation and ask yourself what is it that they are communicating with you. What is it that they are requiring? What do they need? What are they sharing with you? What emotions are there? Be present with them and get very in tune with their needs and their desires, the words they are and are not saying, and the energy behind their words.

If you can provide a way to support them without over-mothering or doing for them, then go ahead. As the evolved mother, we want to step out of doing for other people, but we do want to support them. An unskilled mother jumps in and wants to fix everything, make the pain go away and often times, take away the valuable lesson being offered. A skilled mother supports the other person in finding the strength within them to get what they desire. She can even call upon her High Priestess who knows that everyone has all the power and resources they need within them to overcome any challenge in their life.

Ask yourself how can you support them in the most loving and honoring way? And if you are not sure, you can ask them. The gift of the mother is having an intuitive sense of what they need. This requires that we close our mouth and we open up our ears and hearts and we get present. We are off our cell phone, we are not multitasking, we are not doing one thing while somebody is talking in your ear. This is a challenge for most of us these days. We are listening to our children talking about their day, nodding robotically, not hearing a word because we are scrolling through Instagram, checking emails or thinking about our day at the office. I've never been guilty of this. Well, maybe just a few hundred times, but I try to catch myself. Stop and listen to others, their needs, their desires and their motivations. Listen to what is really going on with their emotions and practice presence, connecting on a deep, intuitive level.

A MOTHER'S INTUITION

I remember countless days where I would get a feeling something was wrong, would walk toward my son's crib and sure enough, he was just about to wake up or needed me for one reason or another. The Mother is extremely intuitive on an energy level. We're going to talk about intuition on two different levels; the Mother's intuition versus the High Priestess' intuition. The Mother's intuition is the energetic connection she has with the people around her. She is sensitive. She is so in tune with others, she can feel the energy that is emanating from people. That is why a mother will be in one room and she knows her child is in need of something in another room. When she is in tune with the people she cares about, a sibling, parent, child or spouse, she can feel when something is off. There are countless stories of this where a woman knew something was wrong, called a sibling and found out they just had a heart attack, even though they are on the other side of the planet. I've heard many more of mothers who knew something was wrong with their child who was stationed in another part of the world. She is so connected, if something happens to them, energetically, she gets an intuitive hit.

This is one level of energy, whereas a High Priestess is intuitively looking beyond the physical. Accessing this information, although not physical, is a tangible thing. The Mother is intuitive and because she has an energetic intuitive connection to the people around her, her energy tends to mix with other people. The beauty of this natural ability is that she understands other people's thoughts, their feelings, their beliefs, what their needs and desires are, and she can anticipate and provide for their needs.

The problem with this is that she becomes so attuned to their needs, and her energy becomes so intertwined with theirs, that she loses her sense of self. We discussed this earlier, and we observed the energetic aspect of this phenomenon. This is why a woman, particularly one who is sensitive or an empath, can lose herself without ever realizing it until she is left depleted. She loses touch with her own feelings, needs and desires. Because of this, the Mother has to learn how to create and maintain a connection with other people without losing connection to herself. She will also need to learn how to disconnect or separate herself from others. We will discuss how to create this separation on an energy level later in this chapter. This is where she also calls on her inner CEO to set boundaries. And even though the Mother in her wants to run to help, her CEO says when it's time to cut the cord.

GIVING FROM THE HEART

The Mother loves to gift. Whereas the Playmate loves to give something beautiful, something fun, something that makes people say wow, the Mother loves giving something thoughtful. She puts a great deal of consideration into what would make a person feel good. The Playmate makes sure the wrapping paper is stunning and has a perfect bow on it. The Mother makes sure the bow is in the person's favorite color. The CEO, while we are at it, is concerned with practicality and duty. She makes sure the gift is something practical that would be used and appreciated. The CEO remembers obligation, so even though finding a gift for her son's mother in law's birthday may not be a top priority for her, she does it because she knows it's the right thing to do. The High Priestess reminds her of that. The CEO is a great trader, she keeps score and remembers things the other feminine types may not be aware of. The CEO in you wants to keep the score even, she doesn't want to feel like she owes anybody anything. She wants to keep the game fair and makes sure that the Mother doesn't overdo it to the point of depletion and martyrdom.

As a woman embodying the Mother archetype, we want to give from the heart, something that is meaningful to the recipient and something that resonates with them. We give, not to get, but to make someone feel special. We know and understand the person we are sharing this special treasure with. We know their likes, we know their dislikes, we understand their preferences and what makes them truly feel cherished. We want to light them up, make them feel great and share something from our heart, right to their heart.

As a Mother, take the time to get to know the people you love and the people you share your life with. This can include your neighbors and co-workers. As you get to know them, pay attention to what they say, trips they've taken, hobbies they have. Pay attention to what makes them light up as they talk. Do they light up when talking about experiences they've had or would like to have? Are there certain tastes that are special to them? What colors do they gravitate towards? Do they always order a bottle of wine from a specific region or melt when you begin to talk about a certain type of food? Take note and when it's time to share a gift, pull this out of your memory and find something that you know they will love. As a bonus, the CEO knows it's a good idea to write it down in a journal that she keeps every day. She jots down things she wants to remember, and she may even begin collecting gifts throughout the year, saving them up for those special occasions.

The Mother is responsible for receiving just as much as she gives, without keeping score. The Mother gives without expecting anything in return. When you give at 1000% and continue to do so, despite feeling tired, depleted, and full of resentment, that's the barometer indicating it's time to pull back. When you want a little something back and it does not come, that is a sign that the mother is drained. But as mothers, we don't give with expectation.

The CEO needs to keep the Mother in check. The CEO reminds the Mother to receive so she can continue to give. She must be open and willing to ask for and receive support, gifts, love, money and everything she needs and desires. We give to our children and those we care about and we don't expect anything back. So the dance is in noticing how you feel. Are you giving a gift, giving from the overflow or abundance, because you want to truly make someone's day and make them feel great, or are you feeling like you are giving, giving, giving and are resenting that you are not receiving anything in return? Do you feel that you are getting taken advantage of and that what you are doing is not appreciated? It's not a tit for tat barometer but rather an emotional barometer. How are you feeling as you gift? Do you feel you are giving or do you feel others are taking? Is it truly from the heart or is it a duty, an obligation or a way to get something? The thing you want doesn't necessarily have to be material. You may give expecting love, loyalty, validation or even praise. There is nothing wrong with that unless you do it unconsciously.

I hear women all the time say I give so much, I need to stop giving. My response to this is as women, we are designed to give. Giving connects us to the overflow of love and abundance we have access to. When we stop giving, we stop the flow and this hurts us more than it hurts others. What is actually happening to so many women is they are not giving, but they are being taken from.

As a child, I remember having to jump up to get my dad a glass of water when he asked. He was content to park himself wherever he was at the moment and send his little helper to wait on him hand and foot. I did as I was told, albeit begrudgingly day after day. I dared not question my dad. When guests arrived, I was taught how to be the good little helper and make sure their needs were met. They were taken care of and had the best seat, the best piece of pie or if they were staying over, they were given my room while I slept on the couch.

I was taught to give. I was trained to give. As I got older, it was just who I was. Eventually, anytime someone around me would simply imply a need, I took it as my cue to jump up and take care of that need. If someone nonchalantly said they were thirsty, I would jump up and get them a glass of water. If someone mentioned they were cold, I would take my jacket off and give it to them. Whatever they needed, I felt it was my obligation to fulfill that need for them. I was trained to hone in on other people's needs more than my own. What I only realized later is I wasn't giving at all. I was being taken.

It's no wonder I was developing a resentment and blocking any channels to receive. I felt like people were taking from me because they had a need and I felt obligated to fill it. I wasn't giving because I truly cared about them. I was giving because I had to, that is how I was taught and that is what I had to unlearn. I had to stop taking on other people's needs and hearing their casual comments as my job to fix or fulfill. Giving from the heart means there is no obligation and there is no requirement that you do so. You give completely from love and abundance because you have a deep desire to share your own overflow of love and abundance. This overflow only comes from receiving. I learned a valuable lesson. I have to receive in order to give.

The hardest part for me to learn was to ignore people's comments when I had no true desire to give. This was true when I felt people were starting to take advantage of me or when I knew if I did take care of them, I would feel resentful. The learning for me was to use specific words such as, help yourself to water, or I'm sorry you are going through that, followed by the question, "what are you going to do about it?". Then the real lesson for me was to shut my mouth and stay put when every ounce of me was programmed to jump to their request, implicit or implied. Thank the universe for the CEO who kept me strapped to my seat.

I have even changed the words I use and now say I am gifting rather than giving. This was shared by a beautiful mentor of mine, Tara Marino. Giving has a charge to it, it holds an element of give and take, meaning when you give, someone is taking. That can light up a negative feeling in you, a feeling like you are being forced to give. It did exactly that for me. Now I use the word gift. It becomes clear to me when I use that word that I am gifting someone something from my heart, no strings attached, no resentment and no expectation. If it doesn't feel like a gift from me, I just don't do it. When it no longer feels like a gift from the heart, then allow your CEO to step in and either pull back on the giving, be aware of your intention behind the giving, or become better at receiving. Receiving is allowing something to come in, being grateful and happy for the gift without any guilt and without feeling like you owe anybody anything.

GIFTING FORWARD

As I shared earlier, the Mother is the giver. Her very nature requires her to take care of other people and "spread the love". There are so many ways to share your abundance and provide gifts to the world. You could go into a Starbucks and buy a drink for the person behind you, pay for the drinks for the person in front of you or even pay the toll for a car behind you. It is such a great feeling to share a special surprise for someone who is not expecting it. Notice how you feel when you give a gift to somebody who isn't expecting it and who doesn't know you. Anonymous gifts can be so fulfilling and fun. Knowing that you just did something for somebody is a beautiful gift to the Mother. Not only does the life of the person on the receiving end get lifted, but so does yours as you give.

I normally would not share a story like the one I am about to as I don't like to talk about my own gifting experiences, but I believe it may offer an idea for you to pass on. One day, I was in Los Angeles by the airport waiting for a meeting that was running really late. I was starving and I had driven up early so I went to look for breakfast. I found an Ihop, sat down and had my breakfast. As I was finishing, I noticed a lady walk in with three big bags. She looked a little unkempt, her hair was wrapped in a big turban and she looked very overwhelmed and tired. I don't know if she was homeless but she did look a little burdened. As I got my check, I asked my waiter to find her waitress and ask for her check. He was a little confused and I just repeated, can I please have her check? He brought the check and I gave him my card. I said, can you put both of them on here? I added, but please don't tell her. He asked emphatically, are you sure? I said yes. He went on again, I'm sure she would want to thank you, let me tell her, let me tell her you paid. I said, no, no, no, please don’t. I literally had to run out of there because he was so adamant about wanting to tell her. I repeated, no, please, I just want to pay.

And honestly, it did not feel like anything extra special. I was just drawn that day to pay for her meal. Even when I left, I did not get a great feeling of satisfaction or a feeling that I did something wonderful. There was no big wave that came over me, it was just a quiet surrender to gifting something that I was being pulled toward. I felt more of a calling, a quiet calling. What I did experience was a beautiful peaceful feeling of wholeness. I felt fulfilled in that moment and that is the gift from the Mother.

GIFTING AND RECEIVING

"A mother's love is the fuel that enables a normal human being to do the impossible."

~ Marion C. Garretty ~

RECEIVING

The capable, independent woman of today finds it very difficult to receive. We deflect gifts, compliments and acts of service. We feel we have to reciprocate and give back to someone who has given to us. When we deny a gift, feel guilty or immediately give something back, we are saying no to the gift and denying the other person's pleasure that they receive when they give a gift. The easiest way to learn how to receive is to begin to allow compliments in. When you receive a compliment, let it land. I know, I know, it's tough, we want to immediately say something back, but resist the urge. In fact, when someone gives you a compliment, simply say "Thank You", that's it, period, full stop, nothing else.

When someone pays you a compliment and you give one right back, you are neither giving nor receiving, you are only trading. If you feel the need to compliment them, save it for a later time. When you compliment someone right away, you are giving back their gift to you. Imagine how horrified you would feel if you realized you just re-gifted something someone gave you. It is as if someone gave you a beautiful scarf and you gave that scarf right back to them. No one benefits from the gift, neither the giver nor the receiver. Make a conscious effort to separate the gifting and the receiving.

The same thing applies to actual gifts and gifts of service. The Mother loves to give but unless it's an appropriate holiday like Christmas or an Anniversary where people exchange gifts, accept the gift graciously and say thank you, with no obligation to give back. If someone gives you a gift or does something nice for you, by all means, show your love and appreciation by gifting them something in return but do it on another day, at another time. In the present, say thank you, be grateful and show your appreciation of the thoughtfulness and the gift by expressing it verbally and with your excitement.

IN THE KITCHEN

I can't help it but I love food. Something about the cozy feeling you get when you've had a long day and you come home to mom who treats you to a snack or even better, something homemade. Food has always been a part of growing up in my culture and in my family. In Egypt, everything revolves around food. I remember the freshly baked apple pie sitting temptingly on a chair by the front door to cool in front of a fan. My brother and I sat there staring at the pie. We were watched closely by mom who threatened us not to touch it until it was ready. It was never ready fast enough. Is it ready yet mom, we would yell every 5 minutes. It seemed like an eternity. But then it passed mom's test. It would not fall apart and had enough time for all the tastes and textures to blend together to create what I still believe is the best homemade apple pie ever, Mom's.

Growing up, knowing mom spent hours in the kitchen to create the best dinner or the most tempting snacks in my younger days, I learned the meaning of nourishment. She spent hours and lots of love and care preparing a meal that would fill her children's and husband's hearts and tummies. She took great care to create beautiful meals for celebrations and guests anytime they came by. My mom cooked every night, we rarely went out to eat and we didn't just throw something in the microwave. The microwave wasn't even a household thing yet. It was during those times that we sat around the table, sharing our day, our stories, laughing and connecting. I felt loved, I felt satisfied, and I felt complete. It's no wonder why so many people equate food with love.

When I owned my restaurant, I had a clear vision of what I wanted to create. I wanted people to have a place to gather, a place that felt like home where they could slow down, have their senses enticed by the gorgeous décor, the delicious food, the beautiful aromas and enjoy being taken care of. I wanted people to come and sit for hours connecting with their family and friends while being nourished with great food and amazing wine.

Too often people guzzle down their drinks and swallow their food without ever really tasting it. I wanted to slow people down, to really taste the delectable food made with care and feel nourished; body, mind and soul. I believe that when food is made with love, that love transfers from the heart, through the hands of the chef and onto the food. This love is tangible and the food tastes significantly better.

COOKING WITH LOVE

During home gatherings, the kitchen always seems to become the hub. What I find most rewarding about cooking is being together in the kitchen-catching up on everyone's lives, talking, eating, drinking, and laughing. My inspiration in the kitchen comes from the pure joy of making others happy. Food really does feed the soul. To amplify your gift of nourishment as the Mother, set the intention that you are preparing love. I promise you, the food will taste different as that love travels from your heart into the food.

Cooking is a gift you give your family every day. If you know how to cook, fabulous. The Mother is the chef of the home, of course with everyone pitching in. I am not condoning being a slave to the kitchen, the CEO would never allow it, and you know I would run away from it. If you don't know how to cook or don't have the time, then have prepared or semi-prepared meals sent to your home. It saves so much time, is healthy and tastes homemade. No matter how hectic your schedule, everyone should sit together regularly. Find time to coordinate your schedule and make it a priority. If you can only gather once per week then commit to everyone being together for that one day. I have only one child so our times together were very special. If you have more than one child, make it a point to spend quality time individually with each of them. They will cherish this time and the memories for years to come.

Those special times and treats you create make the family feel very special and create long lasting memories. I felt very special when my mom made my favorite sweet bread. Today, it is still something that I associate with special occasions and fond memories. Just one bite can transport you back to that moment in time, whether it's the Christmas you spent at your grandma's or the 4th of July camping trip on the beach. When I cook, I feel like I'm providing love and nurturing. It is the most wonderful feeling to express your love in a way that is meaningful and tangible. I love having everyone around the dinner table, chatting and laughing. It makes me feel happy and full. Allow nature to be your inspiration to cook. Use fresh fruit and vegetables all year round. There is no better feeling than to have spent the time planning, preparing and serving a meal that brings smiles to the faces of my family and friends.

This is not just reserved for those who are married or have families. If you are single, host gatherings where people can bring a dish to share. Create a beautiful ambiance and allow time for people to mix, mingle and participate in engaging conversations. When we are around other people, at home, at work, in social situations, food is one area where we can easily nourish and fill each other up; body, mind and soul. The nourishment we get triggers the memories of family, of bonding, of love. Those feelings make us feel closer to the ones we are sharing the meals with.

In the workplace, we can make others feel good and taken care of through food. During my monthly meetings, 20 staff members would have to meet after a long hard day and have to endure an hour of announcements, new procedures, and numerous requests for reports, paperwork and documents, all with nearing deadlines. One thing that made it so much easier for everyone to be there was the food. Plan on adding some sort of treat for employees at work. Progressive workplaces these days like Google and Facebook boast free food. Employees are happier and engaged. You can ask any child and discover that the best treats are the ones unexpected. Randomly fill the employee lounge with fresh fruit. Bring bagels to a morning meeting. Surprise co-workers with freshly baked cookies or store bought ones that pass for home made. Make sure there is coffee or hot chocolate for special occasions or gatherings. This little touch will make people feel special, connected and cared for.

Nine

YOUR BODY

"Motherhood doesn't mean giving up on sensuality, but rather finding new ways to experience and express it. When a mother connects with her body and embraces her sensuality, she is not only nurturing herself but also teaching others the importance of self-love and self-expression."

BRINGING SEXY BACK

Sometimes, as mothers, we can get so absorbed in our roles that we forget about our own sexuality. It's easy to neglect our appearance, stop fixing our hair or wearing makeup, and just focus on our family's needs. But this can make us feel less attractive, less sexy, and less like a woman. It's worth noting that when we neglect our own lives, passion is often the first thing to go. By the end of the day, we're exhausted and have failed to replenish our own energy. We're not turned on, and we don't have the energy to rev ourselves up sexually. Plus, since we're so focused on taking care of everyone else, we don't give our partners the space or time to connect with us sexually. We make it difficult for them, saying no to their advances or simply turning away from their every attempt to get intimate. We forget that we're also human beings with our own needs, and that it's important to take care of ourselves in order to maintain a healthy relationship with our partners.

Women are sexual beings. We are creative beings. Sexual energy is creative energy. Our sexual energy allows us to give birth to new ideas just as much as it allows us to give birth to new lives. As Mothers, we need to stay connected to our sexuality, open up to our passionate nature and allow ourselves to be filled up with this life giving energy.

Gift yourself the time and space and you will find you have more energy to get through your day. You can create simple routines to assure that your needs are met, you are feeling supported and you are giving yourself enough time to rest so that you can open up to and accept the intimacy in your life. Create transitionary times throughout your day. Give yourself space and time in the mornings to take care of yourself, put on something that makes you feel beautiful as well as comfortable and take the time to shower, fix your hair and put on a little makeup every day. Trust me, you will feel better. Have a cup of coffee or tea in the morning and just be with yourself, spend time connecting with you. If you don't have 10 minutes for yourself in the morning then you definitely have some work in resetting priorities. I'm not just talking to you, I'm talking to most women out there who are so busy caring for others that they simply have not insisted that they come first. Between putting the kids to bed and getting yourself to bed, make sure there is ample time for self care and self nurturing. Yes, this may mean stepping into your CEO to enforce a regular bedtime for the kids. No more letting them run the show. And ask for help when you need to create space and time for yourself. Remember the mask on the airplane. . . Ok, let's move on.

THE MOTHER LOAD

I slowly started gaining weight after I got married. After I gave birth, I was a whopping 236 pounds. This was a period in my life where I was fighting to find my place, lost and alone, trying to prove myself and working myself to exhaustion. I truly feel excess weight is the malady of the unbalanced Mother. I was hurting emotionally. I gained weight because I didn't feel good about myself. I gained weight because I didn't love myself. I gained weight because I lost my sense of self and I gained weight because I was protecting myself. Weight was a beautiful barrier, a great way to keep people out of my space and to become invisible. It provided the cushion I needed when I over-gave. It provided the shield I needed when I was too empathetic and took on other people's problems. It provided the barrier my body needed when I had no boundaries. At the end of this chapter, you will learn an energetic tool you can use in your meditations to set your barriers, your boundaries. Creating this barrier will protect your precious space from being drained and keep you from unconsciously wanting to hold on to excess weight.

NO MORE BULLYING

As women, we are extremely critical of our bodies. We judge our bodies, pointing out all its flaws and cursing the parts that don't resemble runway models. We feel awful about ourselves and turn to food. We eat, feel guilty, gain more weight and feel worse about ourselves. It is a vicious cycle. The Mother would never stand for bullying so I invite you to take a stand for any type of bullying, including bullying your body into weight loss. If you packed on a few extra pounds, forgive yourself for the weight gain, forgive yourself for judging yourself, forgive yourself for doing the best you can to protect your space while holding onto all the energy from people around you. There is a difference between bullying your body into weight loss and loving and honouring your body into perfect, healthy weight. The more you love your body, the more you will effortlessly release the weight. Accepting your body as it is, loving all its parts, and being gentle with yourself is key. What you will find is that you begin to treat it better. You begin to listen to it more. You begin to feed it foods that nourish it rather than foods that make it feel heavy and yucky. You will make better choices for your body and get to a place where fresh fruits and vegetables become more loving than sugar rich cakes and sweets that give you an initial high followed by a lingering low.

SLEEPLESS IN SEATTLE OR WHEREVER YOU ARE FROM

It is no secret that mothers suffer from sleep deprivation. But it's not just mothers, women in general require more sleep than men, on average 20-30 minutes per night. Seriously! And while women need more sleep, they aren't getting the sleep they need. Exhaustion from lack of sleep affects so many women yet somehow we have become accustomed to the lack of sleep, pushing through the day and crashing at night from sheer exhaustion. Women are run down by work, taking care of the kids, performing physically, mentally and emotionally taxing jobs all day long and multi-tasking, all of which depletes our energy. Add to the fact that we are running around all day on sheer adrenaline, we treat ourselves to unhealthy, temporarily stimulating foods such as coffee, ice cream and fried foods. Not only are our bodies exhausted, our minds are burdened. Our racing minds control us right before bedtime making it even more difficult to fall asleep. This is usually because this is the first time during the day that we are not "doing" something and our mind can finally run without interruption. Most of us get less sleep than we need and the quality of our sleep is often less than optimal. This leads to irritability, impaired decision making, increased fatigue, addictive behaviors, unhealthy eating habits and depression.

It is difficult to be happy and fully enjoy your day when you start it feeling not fully refreshed. We have to remember that the purpose of sleep is to rejuvenate our bodies and recharge our batteries. I know I can go much longer and accomplish more tasks with joy and purpose when I have had a good night's rest. When my sleep is interrupted or when I have to wake up earlier than I would like, it throws my entire day off. I am not happy, I drag my body through the day and have a difficult time dealing with the physical, mental and emotional charges of the day.

There are a number of things you can do to get good quality sleep. Of course these are only my personal suggestions so please use your common sense and consult your physician or an expert if you have any questions or concerns. Create a routine where you go to bed and wake up at the same time each day. Your body has a miraculous rhythm that can get in sync pretty quickly if we train it. It can support you in falling asleep easily and waking up naturally. Stop eating or drinking 4-6 hours before bedtime depending on your age and metabolic state. Water is okay although I would suggest not drinking water an hour or two before bedtime to avoid getting up in the middle of the night to go to the bathroom.

Create a bedtime ritual where you turn off all electronics including the television, and emails at least 2 hours before bed. Take the first hour to connect; connect with yourself, connect with your family, connect with a favorite book. Use this time to play board games with your family (remember that old favorite pastime before everyone got entrained to stare down at their phones for hours on end). Talk with your family, read your kids' favorite books with them, talk with your spouse about life, your dreams and plans. You can also use this time to pour yourself a cup of relaxing tea, tidy up around the house and plan your next day (more on this in the CEO chapter).

The second hour, slowly work into your bedtime ritual. Journal, visualize your dreams and goals, take a shower or wash up, make love with your spouse and meditate or pray. By the time you hit the sack, you will have turned down your racing mind and you and your body will fall asleep easily and gently.

Most people complain that by the time they get to bed or try to meditate, their mind begins racing. The fact is that your mind has been racing all this time, you have just been adding more noise to drown out this racing mind. The noise of television, social media, running around and keeping busy is an attempt to quiet the mind. Many think sitting in front of a television or scanning through image after image on social media is a relaxing way of turning off the racing mind, but in fact, studies have shown that this causes low levels of stress. Screens are a low grade, on-going source of stress.

By the time you sit and do nothing, you start to hear the chatter going on in between your ears and because this is the first time you give it air time, it starts off loudly. This can be disconcerting. If you ever wake up in the middle of the night with thoughts racing, you definitely are not giving your mind the air time it deserves during the day. The only reason you are getting woken up with thoughts racing is because it's so quiet. This is the only time you can't drown out your thoughts with outside noise. Your subconscious mind says, finally, we can get her to stop and listen. Of course this can be annoying and extremely frustrating. If you suffer from this prevalent condition, my suggestion is start by taking more time to simply sit and watch your thoughts. Don't try to meditate, don't do anything other than sit and observe your thoughts for a while. They may be loud at first, but just like a toddler trying to vie for your attention, as soon as you direct your attention to your thoughts, give it the time and space it deserves, it will calm down and get quieter. Do this every night for one week and you will notice a huge difference in the quality of your sleep.

Ten

YOU ARE NOT BROKEN

"And the moon said to me- My darling, you do not have to be whole in order to shine."

~ Nichole McElhaney ~

FIXING OURSELVES

In my coaching practice, I work with many single women looking for relationships. There is an idea out there, especially in the personal development arena, that states you need to find yourself, to know who you are and to work on yourself, before you get into a relationship. This has kept many well meaning, amazing and powerful women from finding love. This is a sad reality and it is a lie. The fact is we grow through interaction with others. We grow through opportunities to come face to face with other people. Interacting with others shows us our flaws, shows us our strengths, allows us to find parts of ourselves we wouldn't connect with if we were to stay invisible, within the walls of our internal cave. This is how we evolve.

People who are around us who see us in our worst possible moments yet still care for us and still see beauty in us, reflect to us who we are. They demonstrate to us that we are capable of being unconditionally loved, in all of our mess and all of our problems and all of our stuff that needs to be fixed. We are so capable of and worthy of love. We learn we don't have to be perfect to be loved. Needing to be perfect, which affects so many women these days, keeps women from connecting and allowing others in. It keeps women remaining invisible for fear of being seen. This is an epidemic that needs to stop with our generation. Yes, we must be committed to daily showing up as the best version of ourselves, constantly going through life with eyes wide open, conscious, aware and mindfully striving to connect with what really matters. However, you are perfect, you are not broken and you do not need to be fixed.

The people that do not love us, who hurt us and light up the dark places within us are also our teachers and in fact, can be our greatest teachers. They show us our wounds, old hurt we have been hanging on to, places we need to heal, and pictures, limiting beliefs and decisions we have taken on that no longer serve us. Our opportunity is to use this gift, these people and lessons, as a pathway to releasing, letting go and finding our true essence beneath the wounds.

MIRROR

The truth is not that I need to be fixed and then I can find a relationship. We can open up to love and continue to grow through the mirror in front of us. People are mirrors for us. We can easily be happy if we go and meditate on the top of a mountain in a cave somewhere. Why? Because no one's going to piss us off (excuse the language). No one is going to be around us to light us up or ask us to do something that is uncomfortable or show us where we might still be holding onto hurt or have anger or have old lingering emotional baggage that we need to move through. It is in our interaction with others that those things get lit up. The reason they are lit up is because it provides an opportunity for us to grow through these experiences. I once heard someone say the definition of love is giving someone the power to destroy you trusting they won't use it.

Open yourself in a vulnerable way to allow others to see you. The unbalanced Mother seemingly has it all together because she is the worker bee. She is the one that is taking care of everybody. The opportunity here is for your inner Mother to step back and be vulnerable and allow other people to see you and to take care of you. Open up to unconditional love for yourself and allow others to love you in the same way.

EMOTIONS

On an elemental level, water connects you to your Mother energy. The Mother is the emotional part of a woman and is the emotional connection to and from her. When you feel emotions, sadness, fear, anger, hurt or guilt, check in with your inner Mother to discover what she requires or what she is lacking. What does she need in order to feel nurtured and taken care of? Mother yourself and just like a mother would get down to her child's level and connect with her feelings, come into your own center and connect to your feelings. Soothe your inner child. Give her the connection, the understanding, the words or affirmations she needs to hear in that moment.

You can quickly and easily connect with your Mother Feminine type by being around water. Have you ever felt that calm healing energy whenever you are by the ocean? Water is a powerful source of emotional healing and strength. In the shower, revel in that feeling of water pouring over your entire body. Feel the pulse of the water gently massaging your skin. Experience the peace and tranquility of a soothing bath. If you feel as if there is an emotional build up, perhaps you are dealing with something emotionally taxing or are feeling emotional for whatever reason, the ocean or any moving water is beautiful for getting in touch with yourself and that healing, nurturing energy within. Drinking plenty of water is essential. Moving water allows the movement of emotions through and out of you. Hearing the water flow, the sounds of the water crash, bathing in moving water all help your Mother energy. An indoor fountain is a wonderful stress reliever. The natural beauty of flowing water, along with its soothing bubbling sound, calms your mind and lifts your spirits. It promotes the flow of positive energy and rejuvenates you with tranquility, prosperity, and well-being.

YOUR ENERGETIC BOUNDARY

I have discovered a powerful tool that has aided both me and my clients in shedding excess weight and initiating self-care. It involves establishing energetic boundaries. Once you set energetic boundaries, your body no longer has to set physical ones. You can do this by imaging a bubble around you. This bubble encircles you around your body. Your aura is your energetic space about two feet all around you that is designated for you. This is designed to give you space and breathing room. Oftentimes, this bubble is infiltrated by other people, their thoughts, their expectations, their problems and their demands which depletes us. Just outside the edge of this bubble or aura, imagine a big beautiful rose floating in space. Place a picture of you in the rose. Allow this rose to act as a decoy for energy being directed or thrown at you. This is your boundary. Their energy can go into that rose instead of coming into your body. When you can imagine this boundary around you, you can breathe easier and feel more comfortable in your skin. You become less affected by other people and are less likely to feel drained around them.

EXERCISE

One exercise I encourage you to practice regularly is to notice what feels good and what doesn't feel good to you. The things, people or places that are not good for you will create a reaction. Your body will contract, you will feel like you are suffocating, you will feel like there is something pressing into your precious space. When you are connected to your body and you listen to yourself, this will be apparent. When our focus and energy is on everyone around us, it's easy to lose sight of our own preferences, likes and dislikes. A quick game you can play is when you are in a quiet space free of distraction, imagine the bubble around you and notice how well you can breathe, how much space you have and what your precious energy feels like. After you have basked in that for a while, imagine placing someone or something inside your bubble and notice what happens to you. For example, if you are considering moving to a new apartment, place the picture of the apartment inside the bubble and notice how you feel. Do you expand, is there joy, do you feel light? Or do you contract, feel claustrophobic, have an itchy or uncomfortable feeling in your skin? What about a person in your life, perhaps someone you are dating. Place a picture of them in your bubble and notice what happens to your space. When you begin to notice your own reaction, and you can honor your own feelings, you will learn to only allow beautiful, supportive, expansive people, places and things in your life and you will easily let go of the things, and people that bring you down.

MOTHER CONCLUSION

In conclusion, the power of the Mother archetype lies in her ability to give, care, and nurture those around her. Whether it's her children, family, friends, or coworkers, she is the source of support and nourishment, always giving unconditionally. Her emotional intelligence and intuitive nature allow her to anticipate the needs of others, making her an invaluable asset in any relationship. However, it's important to be aware of the potential risks of burnout and exhaustion that can come from neglecting her own needs. By practicing self-care and setting boundaries, the Mother can continue to embody her strengths and fulfill her role as the keeper and protector of all forms of life.

The Mother is about gifting, receiving and connecting with people. The Mother says YES. The Mother is Feminine by nature. This is the emotional part of you, the part of you that connects with another on a heart to heart level. To bring in more of the mother, you'll want to give something; gifts, food, time or anything you feel the people around you would appreciate. You will also want to learn how to graciously receive from others. Learn to simply say "Thank you" without any guilt or need to reciprocate. Other ways to connect with her include listening to music that stirs your emotions, love songs, heart felt ballads, and country songs that tell stories of people's lives. Surround yourself with water, listen to bubbling water or take a swim in the ocean or swimming pool. Create a safe space for people to be open and be vulnerable with you and allow yourself to be open and vulnerable with those you trust.

Ways to get in touch with you Inner Mother

- *Give a gift to someone you care about*
- *Cook a special meal for those you love*
- *Call a friend and allow her to vent without saying anything*
- *Connect with someone whom you know lives alone*
- *Listen to a bubbling fountain*
- *Take a long bath*
- *Walk on the beach, lake or any soothing water source*
- *Listen to someone with the intention of truly understanding them*

PART III

The Sexy *Playmate*

THE PLAYMATE

"The seductress is a master of enchantment, drawing others in with her irresistible charm and magnetic energy."

WHO IS THE PLAYMATE?

The next Feminine type is the Playmate. This is the Sexy aspect of a woman. The Playmate is a fun, sexy, vivacious, flirtatious woman. She is in touch with her physical body and connects with others, both men and women, on a physical level. She is very much about creating physical beauty around her and is usually surrounded by great works of art, stunning furnishings and maintains a dazzling environment. She is radiant, passionate, seductive and has sex appeal. She pays attention to details big or small and has impeccable taste. She knows how to flirt with people, is able to have fun everywhere she goes and laughs out loud on a regular basis. There is a youthful, vibrant quality about her and nothing holds her back. She is a muse and appreciates life. She understands life is about enjoyment, pleasure and delight. She is in touch with her senses, and loves everything sensual; enticing aromas, incredible food, the feel of silk or cashmere against her skin and the firm smooth skin of her lover against her bare body. The Playmate is the woman that is sexy, beautiful and fully alive. She can have fun, laugh out loud and do karaoke even though she can't hold a tune.

Contrary to what it may seem, the Playmate is a masculine characteristic because she is outward focused and puts forth energy into the world to make something happen. She engages with the outside world, the sensual physical world, and brings into her inner world and inner experiences, that which she loves, that which makes her feel good. She has access to this powerful tool and uses it to affect change around and within her. Connecting with your Playmate will make you feel beautiful, sexy, alive and full of joy.

THE BODY

As women, we're so worried about everyone else, we often don't honor ourselves, or our bodies. How often do you allow yourself the simple pleasure of taking the time in the morning to take a great shower and wash your hair using shampoo and conditioners you find lovely and delicious? Or taking those extra five or six minutes to put on your makeup with care, rather than just slapping it on. Do you go into your closet and throw something on that feels "comfortable" read "boring and unflattering" or do you choose an outfit that you feel great in? If you're like most women I know, you jump out of bed, jump in the shower, jump into your clothes and jump in the car racing to work, all the while not being present to yourself, mind elsewhere already planning your day or mapping out strategies to avoid possible disasters at work.

Women fantasize about having their ideal body yet one of biggest ways women sabotage the prospect of having their ideal body is not taking time to honor themselves and care for themselves, like a beautiful piece of jewelry. If you had a beautiful stone or other possession you loved, you would provide great care for it. You would put it in a safe place, touch it with kid gloves, handle it gently and make sure that you keep it from getting tossed around, broken, or destroyed. Caring for your body is the same way. It can be as simple as finding an amazing moisturizer that is really great for your skin. You better believe that it translates into self-confidence. Your body is precious, it carries you throughout your day, allows you to experience life, to create and manifest all you want and to be there for those you love. Stop treating it disrespectfully, throwing garbage in and neglecting it.

I remember sitting at an office one day. I was waiting for an appointment and I overheard two women across from me. One was telling the other about her skin condition, psoriasis. This peaked my interest as I had suffered from psoriasis from my mid twenties. I hated it, my skin would get thick and crusty and very unsightly. I glanced over at her. I saw no sign of psoriasis. No sign of anything similar to the flaky skin I had on my face, the thick red skin around my neck and on my back. I hated it, yet had grown accustomed to it and oftentimes didn't have time to put the prescribed ointment that would assure my clear skin. I didn't have the time? Crazy to think of it. I decided that day to place more emphasis on taking the time to care for my condition. I started putting the ointment to clear my skin then researched ways to naturally heal my condition. Is there something in your health or body that requires your attention? Even it is something minor, pay attention to the cues that tell you your body is not operating at peak condition. You deserve the attention and care. Make the commitment to care for yourself, if it's eating a certain diet, taking care of pesky conditions before they get big or simply not ignoring that nudge that you are not feeling at 100% today. Don't take it lightly and come back into balance immediately.

TAKE YOUR TIME

Sometimes as women, we would never even think about treating other people or even our stuff half as bad as we treat ourselves. The Playmate would never have it. She cares for herself and her body before anybody or anything else. She knows she has to receive so that she can give. Yes, it may seem selfish, but the Playmate knows there is nothing wrong with being focused on the self as long as the High Priestess keeps her ego and her integrity in check.

I've found in my work with women, the persistent idea or myth that women don't have the time for self care. They claim they don't have time for themselves, to take the extra minute to breathe or light a candle or to do something that makes them feel beautiful, as if someone else has set up their life other than them. When someone says, "I don't have the time to exercise, I don't have the time to get my nails done, etc." it begs the question, "Who is in control of your life?" The CEO would never stand for this. Is there someone that has come down and given you this unreasonable schedule? Most of us have an automatic reaction of "everyone is doing my life to me". "The world has put it upon me," rather than shifting our perception, taking full responsibility for our schedules and realizing that we have the power to create more time. I can tell what is important to you by looking at your calendar. What are you devoting time to? From now on, commit to putting yourself and your needs on your calendar first. Take time to care for yourself. We have the power to manage ourselves in terms of time and we have the response-ability to take back our life. The CEO will help you with this as you will see in future chapters.

Twelve

YOUR BODY BEAUTIFUL

"A woman who feels good in her body radiates confidence and sensuality."
~ Elle Macpherson ~

BODY FUEL

What you are feeding, not only your body in terms of nutrition, but what are you feeding your mind and soul? What media are you paying attention to? Are you watching movies or reading magazines, articles or blogs that are centered around health, education and inspiration or are you watching CNN, Constantly Negative News? Who are you spending time with? Jim Rohn says that you are the average of the five people you spend the most time with. You will share the same income, the physical state, and have the same types of relationships as the people whom you spend the most time with. It's not because the money or health is contagious, but it's the thinking that creates the money, relationships or the health that is contagious. Pay attention to what you are feeding your body, mind and soul and make a conscious effort to surround yourself with everything that supports you and where you want to be.

DRESSING FOR CONFIDENCE

Take the time to dress for confidence. I once hired a stylist to help me with my closet, put together outfits and shop for new pieces I could wear. I had no idea how traumatizing this experience would be for me. I was trying to update my wardrobe and the first step was for us to go through every item I had. I was mortified as she pulled out one item after another and with disgust asked me "WHAT IS THIS?" There were oversized sweatshirts with holes in them, pullovers that were fraying at the ends and polyester pants for those days I didn't want to think about what to wear and had a little too much bloating. She held up many loose fitting pants for the morning after a few too many indulgences or for that time of month. It seemed utterly ridiculous looking back, but in the moment, with all sincerity, I answered her, "you know, like for those days when you just want to be frumpy". She looked at me like I was crazy. "Why would you ever want to be frumpy? Get rid of this" she said and so one by one, items were placed in a pile on the floor until I had just a handful of clothes left, four lonely items left hanging in my closet.

I believe we dress how we feel and we feel how we dress. Your energy matches what you wear, so when you dress frumpy, you feel frumpy and when you feel frumpy, you dress frumpy. When you are stepping into your gorgeous goddess self, sorry ladies, but there is no room for frump. You can still have your cute yoga pants and a nice adorable tank top and feel comfortable and not frumpy when you are lounging around your home. But the clothing that makes you invisible is no longer an option for the Goddess you. It's usually our attempt to hide ourselves from the outside world that drives us to throw on these big sweatshirts and ugly sweats that drown us. No more!

SHOPPING YOUR CLOSET

Closet shopping is the most inexpensive way to create an entire new wardrobe, create space for you, get a fresh start and feel beautiful. One of the easiest ways to get in touch with the Playmate is through her outer appearance. Of course, the way to show up as the beautiful goddess that you are is through what you wear. Her closet is full of clothes that make her feel beautiful and special. The Playmate has a closet cleared of shabby clothes and only has items that are beautiful, fun and feel great on.

Years ago, when I was a teacher, I would start the new school year rejuvenated from a restful summer prepared to work with my lovely teenagers and get going on what was always going to be a fabulous year. I found, however, that by the time spring rolled around, when the few months between spring break and summer started to seem like an eternity, I began to look tired and frumpy. I started to grab the first available item hanging in my closet and threw it on without much reflection on style and fashion. It seemed to be the same five outfits. My clothes got yanked out of the closet which was full of random purchases with no thought to current trends, inventory of clothes or fashion sense. The majority of my thoughtless purchases happen to fall under comfy shirts or pant styles I already owned. These random purchases began to take hold of my closet and by late spring, I lost all sight of the items in my closet and even recent purchases I made. I began pulling out the same old, same old, day in and day out to wear to work. What I noticed was that because of the relaxed loose fitting style and shape, I began to feel frumpy and weighed down. I was a bit heavier than what was comfortable. You know how the bigger the purse you carry, the more items you seem to stuff into it? The same happens with clothes and our body. Funny how your body obeys how you feel about it because, low and behold, I began to fit right into the baggy shapeless shirts that once covered my abdomen, buttocks and waist.

Now I catch myself. When items seem to find itself in never-never land and disappear to the black hole of my closet, I realize it's time to shop my closet. I find an afternoon when I am mentally and physically prepared to go through and wear each and every item. I begin by wearing the most comfortable best fitting bra and underwear. Next, I clear everyone out of the house. Once my boyfriend gave me a hard time every time I took on a task that involves clothes, fashion or "honey does my butt look big in this?" So to avoid any issues and added stress, I just kicked him out. I try on every single item, and with a large mirror, ask myself if I would buy this item again. Does this top look fabulous on me, does it fit who I am today, does it make me look and feel beautiful?

Begin to pare down the closet and find what works for you. You can then create 4 piles, keep, alter, give away and throw out. I have put together great outfits from items I forgot about so I am reluctant to throw things out immediately and have added a transition pile as well. I have many theories on clearing out closets from a de-cluttering sense which is beyond the scope of this book but for now, you decide what you would like to do with your clothes. I know some people are reluctant to throw things away and I know many experts send out a blanket statement to throw or give it all away. I have heard of many women who have read books on organization and have thrown away items they later realized would be perfect with a certain tweak or new season. I know I know, so many people prescribe to the "just get rid of it" "Kondo" principle but I, along with many a friend and client have wanted to wear something we knew we had, only to remember with regret that we threw it out. You have my permission to create a transitional space. It can be a closet, a drawer, a box or a suitcase where you can place items you are not 100% sure you are done with.

I try to pair transition items with something unexpected and sometimes have surprised myself. I once had a cropped black velvet jacket with short sleeves that I could not for the life of me make work in any manner. I was wearing a white tank top one afternoon cleaning the house and had to run down to answer the door bell. I grabbed the jacket to throw over the tank and was amazed how adorable and chic it looked. I threw on jeans and found a sexy new outfit for myself. What I've also done is any t-shirts and tank tops that no longer look divine on me for a night out, I relegate to my work out wardrobe. This little technique has upped the ante on my workout attire and motivated me to get to the gym more often now that I could look cute while getting fit.

Nowadays, I shop my closet every season. It's amazing the new types of outfits I start to think about that work, like last year's blouse underneath my new sweater, wow, I never thought about wearing it like that before. What I also find is that when you put on clothes that have been sitting in your closet, you get a feel for what your body is like in this moment because your body changes. If you are like me and most women I know, you tend to have a range of 2-3 sizes depending on time of month, season and current habits. Most women tend to wear the same 10-20% of the clothes in their closet because it is comfortable and they know what to expect when they wear it, how it will fit, how it will look, how it will feel. But since we change all the time, we need to re-examine the possibilities and expand our options.

Try on every item, get a feel for what makes you feel good, looks great on you and makes you feel fabulous. Ask yourself if you would buy that item today. If the answer is yes, then organize it beautifully in your closet. If not, put it away. Have fun creating new outfits with what you have and you'll soon find that you have more pieces than you need. A bonus tip is to take pictures of yourself in new outfits you've put together. That way when you "run out of things to wear", an enigma only us women understand even in a sea of clothes, you can pull out your look book and look fabulous any day of the week.

FABULOUS AND FRENCH

French women who have reputations for being extremely stylish, have a very small closet compared to the Western woman because they choose quality over quantity. They have a great skirt that can go with several of their blouses and a fabulous pair of shoes that work with many outfits. Be discriminate when you go shopping and look for quality and classic pieces. As you get dressed each day, take the time every morning to wear things that make you feel attractive, beautiful and sexy. If you leave your home looking like a million bucks, you will feel like a million bucks. The bonus is you will attract elevated people, ideas and resources to match the energy you are putting out.

This includes nightgowns, what you where to go to bed, and lingerie. When you are wearing something underneath your clothes, the intimates, it is just as important to make sure they look and feel fabulous. There's something extremely erotic about walking around during the day knowing that underneath your business suit or jeans, you are wearing a beautiful lacy red thong that nobody can see. You stand taller, more confident, you carry an air of mystery because you have something sexy and powerful only you can see. There's an allure that you have, and I promise you ladies, others will notice. One caveat, the lingerie and nightgown or pajamas you wear must feel sensual and beautiful on your skin, and must be comfortable to wear. None of this scratchy stuff or pulling out wedgies all day.

I once bought a really beautiful pink sweater but every time I put it on, it felt very irritating to my skin. I was uncomfortable and felt irritated which defeated the purpose of the gorgeous top. I finally got rid of it and realized how something felt and fit was just as important as how it looked. The same goes for a beautiful dress or outfit that doesn't quite fit right. Either get it tailored, get a great comfortable set of spanx or pass on it. Having tailored great fitting clothes is a must for the Playmate. And once you clear out the old, commit to shopping mindfully. As you go shopping, make sure you are in a positive, self loving state of mind. Try on clothing and ask yourself if this item truly brings out the best in you. Will it elevate how you feel, how you look and your personal brand? Is it aligned with who you are and are you in love with the piece? If not, put it away. You don't need it and it will not bring any value to your life.

ADORNING YOUR BODY

The Playmate loves her body and the way beautiful jewelry and clothes look and feel on her skin and body. If you walk into a museum, you'll notice everything is adorned gorgeously. Items are well taken care of and framed so as to highlight the best features. Your body is just as gorgeous so it should be treated and adorned as such. Getting in touch with your playmate means wearing pretty colors that you're inspired by, gorgeous jewelry that enhances your outfit and beautiful shoes. Anything that inspires you and brings out your exquisiteness. A Playmate is there to impress herself but also loves to enjoy a life that includes others. Although she knows the power of attracting others with her physical appearance, she doesn't do it for other people and she doesn't do it solely for a response.

She wants to feel good in her own skin. The nice thing about adornments is that it doesn't matter how much you weigh, what time of the month it is or how much sodium or chocolate you had the night before. Jewelry always fits and looks fabulous. The same goes for a great pair of shoes or a handbag. (I tried explaining this to many a man but somehow, they still don't get our obsession). When you have a great pair of shoes or earrings you love, or even a gorgeous handbag, all you need to do is put them on and you will feel beautiful. This beauty will reflect from the inside out. When you feel beautiful, you start to make choices that are in alignment with how beautiful you feel. You will naturally begin to make better choices for you. You will turn down that second piece of chocolate cake, you will dump the man that makes you feel unworthy and you will spend less time with friends or family members that weigh you down with their negative judgemental words.

Thirteen

SELF CARE

"A woman who takes good care of herself and prioritizes her self-care rituals exude a radiance that cannot be matched. When you nurture your body and mind, you tap into a well of confidence and sexiness that can take your breath away."

SPA BLISS

We can't talk about the Playmate without talking Spa ladies. In today's hectic world, giving yourself a spa day is the ultimate treat, yet a spa day is one of those no longer nice to have but must have for the Goddess. The spa is a place for healing, restoration, connecting with the self and pampering. We spoke earlier about connecting with the Mother through water. Spa comes from the Latin phrase salus per aquae which translates to "health through water." The curative powers of mineral waters and hot springs is famous for its healing powers. At a time when western medicine offered very little in the ways of cures, people would travel to the springs for the treatment and relief of their diseases and ailments. The spa is a source of healing and relaxation and not only is this great for the Mother, healing her on an emotional level, it is very validating to the physical body, for the Playmate and allows her to luxuriate in taking care of herself. Taking the time to get quiet, connect with the temple of the body, allows the High Priestess the time and space to feel whole and fulfilled, let go of the stress of the world that the CEO carries and reconnect to her spirit.

Your challenge, should you choose to accept it, is to create space for a spa day at least once a month. Carve out the time to take care of your body, luxuriate in the senses, and disconnect from the world. There are many options depending on your budget including giving yourself a spa day at home and finding low cost spas in your area. Many hotels offer day passes where you can use the pool, steam room and sauna. You can even get together with a girlfriend and give each other facials, manicures and loving attention.

DELIGHT IN THE SENSES

The Playmate is extremely sensual and is in touch with her sense of taste, smell, touch, sight and hearing. She revels in the smell of gorgeous perfume and scented candles. Scents have a different effect on different bodies. Take the time to find your signature scent, something you love and wear it often. The Playmate only wears perfume or body lotion that makes her feel beautiful and sensual.

The Playmate enjoys life, everything fun and everything sensory. Take the time to breath deeply during your daily activities, whether it's a night out dancing or doing laundry. Only choose sensual elements that are pleasing to you. The feel of gorgeous silk or cashmere against her skin puts her in a state of pure bliss, and listening to soothing music takes her to another place. You are worth feeling great every moment and delighting in soul serving music.

HEAD TO TOE CARE

Taking care of her entire body is an important aspect that the Playmate values highly. Let's make taking care of yourself a fun and exciting adventure! It's not about looking like a supermodel, but it's about feeling confident and radiating your best self. And where does it all begin? With good hygiene, of course! Your hair should be clean and smell amazing because let's face it, others will notice if it doesn't. If you're not a fan of daily washes, no problem! Use a dry shampoo to absorb any unwanted smells. Take the time to nourish your hair with quality shampoo and conditioner or make your own home masks to keep your locks healthy, shiny, and strong. Experiment with different styles that make you feel beautiful - even that just-rolled-out-of-bed look can be stunning when it's done right. Sorry ladies, but that messy hair look is not the same as the "I really did just get out of bed" look.

Achieving great skin is not just about appearances, it's about promoting overall health and wellness. Great skin is a sign of youthfulness and vitality. If you're experiencing skin issues like dryness, oiliness, or breakouts, it could be a sign of an imbalance. Take the time to figure out the root cause. Maybe you need to switch up your skincare routine or look at your diet to identify potential triggers. Hormonal imbalances or allergies could also be to blame. By addressing these underlying issues, you'll not only improve your skin but also boost your confidence and sense of well-being. To maintain healthy skin, make sure to wash your face every morning and night, apply sunscreen and moisturizer to protect it from pollutants, and toxins in the air. Don't forget to brush your teeth twice a day, floss regularly, and address any issues like bad breath, which could be a sign of an underlying problem. Remember to shower every day and stay fresh and clean, paying special attention to your intimate areas. By prioritizing your personal hygiene, you'll radiate confidence and feel your best every day.

Deodorant is a must and if you insist on not using a deodorant (I understand the harsh chemicals may be a deterrent) then you definitely need to shower more often, perhaps twice a day. For those that do not use deodorant because of the toxins, you should pay close attention to what you feed your body. If you feed it toxins, your body will emit unpleasant odors through your pores. At that point, you might as well use a good deodorant. If you are absolutely certain you are eating clean, you may not emit a scent as you perspire.

You should be well groomed and look as put together as the occasion warrants. If you are running to the grocery store, no need to curl your hair but perhaps putting your hair in a ponytail makes you look and feel put together. Keep your nails clean and manicured and keep your skin moistened with lotion to prevent premature, dry, aging skin.

PRIORITIZING YOUR WELL BEING

A Playmate's health is of high priority. She knows how sexy she feels when she has energy, vitality, and health. She loves it when clothes fall on her body beautifully and when she has the stamina to keep up with her children and play for hours on end without feeling the need to stop and rest. She appreciates that she can walk up a flight of stairs and not feel winded. Not to mention being able to sustain hours of pleasure that gratify her sexual desires. She can laugh and join in on all the excitement around her and participate in all adventures, big and small. To the Playmate, it is not okay for her to feel too tired to engage in life and all its wondrous experiences. She would never tolerate an inability to keep up with fun activities that make her feel alive. Health is no longer a nice to have, nor is it about vanity, but rather, it is essential to the Playmate and the Goddess. Although this isn't a book specifically about health, there are a few tips I have found work wonders for me and my clients. Of course, use common sense and consult with your physician before making any changes.

Fourteen

FLOW

"Take a deep breath, sway your hips to your favorite song, sip some water and give your body the love it deserves. It's amazing how just a few simple self-care practices can make you feel sexier, stronger and more confident."

H2O

The first is water. Approximately 60% of an adult human is made of water. Almost every cell in the body requires water to function properly. Water helps to maximize physical performance, increase motivation and make physical and mental activities feel much easier. It improves mood, concentration and overall energy. And the best benefit is that water can help you lose weight. It increases satiety and boosts your metabolic rate. I drink a liter of water as soon as I wake up, which helps me eliminate everything I was holding onto from the previous day.

I have found that drinking 2 cups of water 30 minutes prior to each meal works great and gives me more energy, helps me to feel cleaner and leaner, makes me less hungry and more satisfied, and improves my digestion. While on that note, only drink water during your meals if you absolutely must. Drinking water while eating tends to dilute your stomach's reservoir of hydrochloric acid which is essential to break down food properly. I found that chugging water with my meal leads to poor digestion and uncomfortable bloating. Of course, check with your doctor about caring for your body, but if you stay hydrated throughout the day drinking between meals, you won't need to chug water with your food.

In the East, hot or warm water is the go to drink of choice. If you think about it, when you have toxins or dirt you want to wash off your hands or body, what is more effective, washing with cold or warm water? Ever since I was a kid, I was taught to wash my hands with warm water. When you think of it this way, drinking warm water seems to make much more sense in clearing out your insides.

Experts will tell you to drink half your body weight in ounces of water. For example, if you weigh 140 pounds, drink 70 ounces of water or the equivalent of about 8½ cups. Make water your go-to drink. Coffee, which can be dehydrating and juices which contain lots of sugar don't count. And I'm not going to even mention sodas… as Nancy Reagan used to say, "Just say no". If you must drink coffee (guilty) or alcohol, commit to drinking one glass of water for every cup of a dehydrating liquid above and beyond what you need to drink. And for those who want to argue that you'll be going to the bathroom all day… Great!! Who wants a sink that's backed up? And when you look down after a run to the bathroom, the waste should be light, not dark. The Playmate does not want that heavy hangover most people feel after eating a meal. Going to the bathroom, getting rid of those toxins in the body, is a good thing and drinking plenty of water makes that process so much easier. Your Playmate will love the way you feel. You will feel light, energetic, flexible and so ready to play and have fun all day long. Your CEO will love it because you will be clear headed and ready to take on the day and all its challenges, and your High Priestess will love it because you will be a clearer channel for higher guidance and intuition.

LET'S ROCK AND ROLL

Making health and exercise a priority is essential for the Playmate. Exercise every day. Yes, I said every day. In my travels to Europe and Asia, I found that people walk everywhere. Yet in so many parts of the United States, we fight for the closest parking space to the gym and will drive to the other end of the mall rather than walk. This is madness. Use every opportunity to walk, dance, play, and move your body. Your playmate will love you for it. Giving yourself the opportunity to move, stay agile and flexible, to get your heartbeat up and get strong, gives the Playmate so much more freedom as she plays in your life.

Women need different kinds of exercise. Women need to lift weights. Yes, lift weights, and I'm not talking about bulking up. In addition to building muscular strength, weight lifting helps women build bone density and prevents osteoporosis which primarily affects women. A Harvard study showed that more than 8 million women versus 2 million men suffer from osteoporosis, a loss of bone mass, which contributes to an increase in fractures. Remember when your grandmother fell and broke her hip? Yeah, don't let that happen to you.

Not only does having a variety of physical activity options provide fun and diversity to your playmate, it also helps you maintain optimal health, physique, energy and overall fitness. When I took a yoga class for the first time, I was working muscles I didn't even know I had. When I took salsa dance lessons, I worked out my thighs in areas squats couldn't reach. Rock climbing helped me work out my upper arms, legs and core. Kayaking helped me build my upper back strength and work out big and small muscles that are hard to get to in the gym. Opt for more variety in developing physical fitness. Your future self will thank you for it.

YOUR TEMPLE

The Playmate only gives her body food and drinks that make her feel fabulous, that is made from the highest quality ingredients and tastes amazing. She would never think of going to a fast food restaurant to eat something that makes her feel yucky, sluggish and sick but rather, she will savor the beautiful fresh fruits and vegetables, or steak and seafood, or any beautiful food she enjoys.

I was at a meeting recently and in walked a colleague who had just had a baby. I complimented her on looking so amazing, getting back to her pre-pregnancy body in a short period of time. I went on to describe how it took me years to take off the baby weight. Even 5 years after giving birth, I was still blaming my weight on my pregnancy. I asked her for her secret. She described the demands of motherhood, how she didn't even have the time to eat, and how she was never one to just eat on the go. She said that if she couldn't sit down and enjoy her meal, she didn't want to be bothered with it. What a beautiful way to honor yourself and your body.

The Playmate knows her worth and strives to treat her body the way a high valued woman would treat it. You would never fill a Ferrari with cheap low octane gas. When you have a gorgeous high performing vehicle, you only fill it with the best maximum octane fuel that keeps the vehicle running at the highest level. For the Playmate, it is essential that she treat her body like a high performing, high valued machine and only feed her body with the best, highest quality, sensually pleasing food and drinks. The Playmate enjoys the pleasure of fabulous food that is only made with the best, freshest, healthiest ingredients.

Her desire when she sits down for a meal is to engage all her senses. When she eats, she doesn't waste her time or fill her body with crap. Only the best will do for her. She only indulges in the finest ingredients and the best foods. When she chooses chocolates, she only chooses the best dark chocolate that melts in her mouth. Her chosen indulgence is gorgeous without preservatives or ingredients she can't pronounce. Whole and unprocessed foods is what she reaches for. And . . . only eat what you truly want and desire, not what you think you should have.

I had dinner with a slender friend of mine. I've struggled with weight for most of my life so of course I asked her how she stays so skinny. What she said was the best thing I've ever heard. "I don't think that much about food" she shared. "I eat when I'm hungry and stop when I'm not". Wow, so simple, yet what a concept. I reflected on my life. When did I stop listening to my body? When did I start obsessing about what I needed to eat and how much, weighing food when on a particular diet and trying to cut out or add certain foods depending on the diet of the year. I had an obsession, spent hours thinking about what I wanted to eat, what I was going to eat, what I should and shouldn't eat and what the next meal will be like, even while I was eating a meal in front of me. I heard a health guru once say that no person who is truly fit and healthy has ever gotten that way from a diet. They get that way from a lifestyle. The lifestyle comes from a commitment to making your love for yourself and your body priority over the temporary high you get from addictive foods that don't make you feel good.

BREATHE DARLING

If you look around at a restaurant, or even pay attention to yourself at meals, you will find that most people don't even breathe when they eat. Make a conscious effort to slow down, breathe and be present while you are eating. The High Priestess will remind you of this. When you commit to honoring and paying attention to your body and what it desires, staying in the present in every moment and throughout every bite, your body starts to get back into alignment. You start to eat consciously and you begin to notice what foods feel good and what foods don't. You notice when to start eating and you notice when you have had enough. The Playmate is not motivated by discipline. As I was writing this, I was curious about the word and looked it up. According to the Oxford Dictionary, "discipline" is the practice of training people to obey rules or a code of behavior, using punishment to correct disobedience. Ugh, punishment is not for the Playmate, she is all about pleasure, no pain. So . . . no obsessing, no discipline around cutting out foods, no counting calories, just simply getting in alignment with your body and opening up the communication between you and your body. Of course, if you are so out of whack, as I have been in the past, and need to recalibrate your body since it is currently asking you for greasy, unhealthy foods, then by all means, charge your CEO with the task of creating a plan and sticking with it. However, once you are back in alignment, you can trust your gut and your palate to crave what it needs and desires. Your body will love it and you will reap the rewards of health, vitality, energy and beauty.

Fifteen

HER JOY

"True beauty comes from finding joy in life's simple pleasures and experiencing them fully. When a woman finds joy in her life, she radiates with an inner light that shines for all to see, and she becomes truly fulfilled and beautiful."

HER ENVIRONMENT

The Playmate enjoys great works of art, exquisite décor, fresh flowers and harmony. She abhors a cluttered, disorganized and dirty environment and her environment is nothing short of spectacular. Anything messy, unattractive or tacky is not aligned with the playmate. She pays attention to details, big or small. And her tastes are impeccable. The CEO and the High Priestess will be determining what specifically is important to her and the playmate makes sure that she's surrounded by what she loves.

Your home, or office for that matter, is your castle. Look at your environment and ask yourself the following questions. Does it bring me joy? How do I feel in this space? Does everything I see, smell and feel energize me? I have a policy that if something is not beautiful to look at, it gets put away in a drawer, closet, box or something else that keeps it hidden. Lay out the gorgeous throw blankets across your sofa. The functional ones that don't look gorgeous get put in an ottoman or some other storage space. Are you lighting candles that make your room smell like joy or do you "save" all those great candles for some day. Pull them out and light them. Pull out your nice china and use them, even for dinner for one. I buy fresh flowers every week and I can tell you, it puts a smile on my face every time I walk into the rooms with the flowers. I planted roses in my yard so I now have the option of picking them directly which is a great alternative to save money. And remember, less is more. When clearing out and decorating your space, remove every item and place one gorgeous item out at a time asking yourself if it still looks beautiful.

LAUGHTER MAKES THE HEART GROW STRONGER

Remember LOL, is that still a thing? It is crucial for the Playmate to burst out laughing every once in a while! Not only is it great for the soul, but it also has several health benefits. So go ahead, find something hilarious, and let out a boisterous belly laugh. We require the oxygen to move through our body. An important key to your own fabulousness is identifying your desires; what brings you joy, what makes you come alive and what makes you so full of light that you laugh out loud with glee. I ask women all the time, "what do you do for fun" and am floored and frankly saddened to find that most women just don't know. When I ask women, "what brings you joy, what would you love, what is fun for you?", there is always such a long pause, followed by a resigned and surprised "I don't know". They are so disconnected from their playful side, they have forgotten what makes them laugh, feel light and brings joy. Women don't even know what they want. We have been so far removed from enjoying pleasure and joy because we have been busy taking care of business and everyone else. Having fun, connecting with what really gives us life seems like such a perplexing question.

To get back in touch with our inner Playmate, we need to ask ourselves this question, and we need to ask and answer it often. I invite you to ask yourself right now, "What brings you joy? What sounds like a lot of fun?" Think about that five-year-old girl within you; that girl that is playful and loves adventure and excitement, even if it means getting dirty and even if it means getting sweaty.

As we get older, we get too practical and we start to think about the consequences of everything. I have curly hair, which equates to high maintenance. And by high maintenance, I mean I have to wash it every single day. In the morning I apply layers of product and it's really crunchy and hard. And if I'm lucky, about eight hours later, there is a window of time where it starts to look good. I cannot blow dry my hair and can't sleep on it because I lose the nice ringlets that form. If I am in a hurry because I have somewhere to go early in the day and I don't have eight hours to fix my hair, I will roll down the windows in my car and blow dry it on my drive. That is the only place that I can blow dry it. So that being said, whenever I think of water, I think of my hair . . . and it's way too much trouble. It's too much of a hassle. Rain scares me and any sign of humidity makes me run for the hills, indoors of course. I don't want to get it wet because then I am going to have to work at fixing it and go through the whole ritual again.

I was on vacation with a group of friends recently and we were by the pool. Well, I was by the pool and they were all in the water having fun. They kept calling me to join them and I just nodded, said I was fine and said I fixed my hair, can't get it wet. I had already washed it for the day and was letting it dry for our evening out. We had plans for a fancy dinner and I wanted to make sure my hair would dry by then and look halfway decent. I didn't want to have to wash it again and definitely didn't want to have to put product on again. It was too much work.

After about an hour of noticing how much fun they were having and how much I was depriving myself on my own vacation, I finally got over myself and got in the water. And I had the best time. Water is something I absolutely love. I revel in feeling the water around me, being soaked in it, floating and swimming in it. I love putting my entire head down all the way into the water and holding my breath and feeling peacefulness and joy. I love splashing around in water and I love putting my head under the waterfall, letting the water give me a gentle head and shoulder massage.

I almost denied myself this pleasure because of the hassle, but no more. Think about some of the things that you absolutely love. What are the things that bring you joy? What brings out your inner five year old or what did you love to do when you were five? It could be dancing, going to a comedy club, watching a funny movie, going on a hike, tickling your child, riding roller coasters, riding a bike, being outdoors, playing in water, or playing other sports. Possibilities are endless.

Pleasure is 100% important to the body; to validate the body. Physically we require pleasure. Because of stress, women have adrenals that are shot. Cortisol levels are consistently high. The results: we are tired, our metabolism slows down and we add unwanted pounds. It keeps us from having energy to get through our day and starts to shut our whole body down. Cortisol is the response mechanism to stress that gets released when we are in fight or flight mode. The problem with most women is that we are constantly in fight or flight mode throughout the day. There are so many fires to put out, hundreds of plates spinning, and a million and one things that we take responsibility for and it is literally killing us. Stress can contribute to heart disease, the number one killer of women nowadays, high blood pressure and a myriad of other health problems. We are killing ourselves because we are forgetting to take care of ourselves.

Joy is the antidote to that. What happens when we are having fun, when we are laughing, when we are dancing, when we are enjoying the pleasures in life, is we release nitric oxide. Nitric oxide blocks cortisol from being released. Joy is not a nice to have, when I have time. We require it on a daily basis. It is time we make it a priority in our life.

Your task, should you accept it, and I hope to gosh you would, is to create a list of those things that sound fun, that you would love to do, that makes you giddy inside just thinking of it. Write it down and continually add to it. This is a list you can refer to on those days where you are so disconnected from your self that you can't come up with anything. Daily, I invite you to choose something to do from the list that is fun. You will also refer to this list when you are rewarding your inner CEO for all her hard work. If you don't take care of that little girl inside of you, she won't give you the energy to continue working toward your big goals. But more about that in the CEO section.

FLIRTING

Women are made to flirt. Women have a unique ability to bring a beautiful, validating energy to people around them, lifting them up and making them feel great about themselves. And while it's often thought of as something only reserved for interactions with the opposite sex, flirting can be so much more than that. Flirting is about truly seeing another person, seeing the qualities that make them special and unique, and making it known to that person. Flirting is about making somebody feel great, powerful, handsome, or beautiful, regardless of gender. And the best part? Flirting isn't just about making others feel good; it's also a fabulous way to reconnect with your own beauty and confidence.

A while ago after my divorce, I was feeling pretty awful about myself. I felt fat and ugly and had an extremely low sense of self-worth. After sitting in this depressed state for far too long, I knew I had to snap myself out of it. At one point, I made a conscious decision to be more generous with my compliments. I realized I was lacking a recognition of beauty around me and thus was blind to it in myself. I was numb to all the wonderful things in my life because I was so wrapped up in my own misery, my own problems and was feeling completely rejected and depressed. I realized I wasn't recognizing beauty in myself and around me. It didn't feel good for me to stay in this place so I decided to turn things around. I chose to pay attention to all the splendid things around me and purposefully began to look for beauty in my environment and to share what I noticed aloud.

I started to compliment everything that I found attractive, beautiful and admirable. It was as simple as complimenting a woman on her beautiful eyes or a man on his great tie. I told attractive women that I thought they were gorgeous. Everywhere I went, I admired the great care received by an attentive waiter or the extra bit of information supplied by the DMV representative. Watching people light up from my simple words encouraged me to ramp up my efforts. I was constantly giving compliments everywhere I went.

Immediately after I began my new ritual, I was waiting for a table at a restaurant and a man came up to me, he gently touched me on the arm and he said excuse me, I just have to tell you, you are stunning. I was so taken aback by this and completely touched by his gesture. After composing myself, I said wow, thank you so much. I'm sure he noticed my own light shine brighter and the smile that said he made my day.

MULTIPLYING YOUR GIFT

So what happened? On that day, I learned the power of giving what you desire to receive the most. This not only makes you feel great and fulfilled, but it also helps you realize that you already possess everything you need or want within you. You can access it anytime, and you are full, brilliant, beautiful, and abundant.

When we can see a quality in others, we begin to reflect that in ourselves. I believe everyone is a mirror. Because I was noticing beauty around me, I was in essence becoming that which I recognized. When you give a gift, that gift multiplies. When you are able to see beauty in someone, you ae actually seeing the beauty in yourself. As you see kindness in others, you are able to see the kindness in yourself. When you are able to see the strength, or the glorious nature of somebody else, you are able to see that in yourself. Everything around you is a reflection and you are saying hello to your own gifts and to the beauty and power within you. Your gift begins to multiply exponentially.

When you do that, it's as if I were to hand you a $100 bill. I would assume you would be happy with that, right? The beauty of this is that when I hand you the $100, I get to keep mine. And you now have the ability to share your $100 bill with someone, to pass it on, make someone's day and magically, you get to keep the $100 as well. And so it is with the Playmate, she makes people feel good and other people want to make her feel good in return. They then pass it on and they pass it on and you get the point. I can't even begin to tell you how many hotel upgrades I received just by walking up to the counter and asking how are you, and saying you have a beautiful smile. Of course I don't do it in a manipulative way, I genuinely recognize and see people for who they are inside. I'm just happy to be there, and happy to have someone kind to me. I make it a point to share my gratitude with them.

I do the same thing at the grocery store. How often do we go to the grocery store, pay for our groceries, put our money away and quickly murmur a hasty thank you as we turn & walk away without ever making eye contact? When was the last time you looked up and made eye contact with the checker and said hello, a real spirit-to-spirit hello, silently saying I see you and think you are fabulous. You become extremely attractive and guess what, everything starts to become attracted to you; people, resources, money, gifts, and compliments. Everything starts to flow towards you, because you are radiating a beauty and abundance that truly is tangible and magnetic.

People in India have a beautiful greeting, Namaste. Namaste means the light of God in me honors the light of God in you. And that goes for everything, the beauty in me honors the beauty in you, the kindness in me honors the kindness in you. Send the silent greeting to people you encounter every day. Include yourself in this silent prayer. Every time you pass a mirror, look yourself in the eye, wink at yourself, and say hello gorgeous, out loud, unless of course there are other people around. You might have some "splaining" to do. Start saying hello to yourself. Whenever I have to write a note to myself, I always begin it with "hey gorgeous".

I encourage you to take on this challenge, notice the beauty around you and verbalize it to those with whom you come into contact. Smile and flirt with everybody. Whenever you see anybody, be it the grocery store clerk, the mailman or your husband, flirt with them, talk to them, share something light hearted or positive. Make a conscious effort to see them, recognize them and say hello to them in whichever way you are inspired. Even if it is just a bright smile, you can say hello, good morning, good afternoon, nice to see you, or even a sincere thank you. Make a commitment now for yourself to slow down, take a second to connect with people, make eye contact, smile, acknowledge people and notice how that positive energy comes back to you.

SEXUAL TRAUMA

"Trauma creates change you don't choose. Healing is about creating change that you do choose."

~ Michelle Rosenthall ~

TURNING DOWN YOUR SEXUALITY

Elementary school had taken its toll on my self-esteem. Lots of girls seemed to be able to sail blissfully through childhood, but unfortunately I was painfully aware of what I was missing when Judy, my new BFF dumped me overnight for the attention of all the 3rd grade boys. Sometime in the middle of 3rd grade, she developed breasts, all the boys noticed and I suddenly became invisible. I was invisible to all the boys and to Judy whom I thought was a friend, all over a couple of bumps. The pressure I felt to make myself sexually attractive was incredibly intense and the harsh truth that sexuality equaled friendship was something I couldn't comprehend at my young innocent age.

Fast forward a few years, I was 13 years old, had just entered high school and was feeling very grown up. I was a late bloomer so hadn't really felt like a woman until late 8th grade, so as I began high school, I was on a mission to reinvent myself as the sophisticated worldly, sexy woman I knew was being cultivated inside of me while I was blossoming. I attended an all girls' catholic high school which meant wearing hideous green and black checkered uniforms that had to fall below the knee. It was picture day and having been forced to wear a school uniform everyday for the last nine years in Catholic school, I was ecstatic that the nuns allowed us to express ourselves through our own wardrobe to take school pictures. Free dress day was a coveted day in high school when we really got to show off a little of our own identity, our personality. Going to an all girls' school didn't offer too many opportunities to "show off" to the opposite sex . . . during school that is, but as soon as the bell rang, the show was on. Boys were lined up outside, most days around the block, that is, if Sister Gerarda was on duty chasing the boys away. There was always the opportunity to get attention from a cute boy on the way home. I conveniently had to meet my brother at the boys' Catholic high school 15 minutes away so I made sure I looked great for the picture and "ahem", myself.

I loved clothes and I would often design dresses and other clothing items. I was blessed to have a very nurturing and craftsy mom who would design and sew them for me. She made the pattern using my drawing, and we would venture off together to the fabric store to choose the color and texture. She would take it home and sew it for me. I was very excited that I had the chance to sit down with her and design my own drop dead gorgeous couture dress. I got busy designing the perfect white dress I was in love with for my pictures freshman year. This one would bring out my olive skin and dark hair. It had a low V-neck with a flap in the front and back that was connected by a band, a little strip of material across the top so as not to look too cheap and seductive. The sleeves were short and puffy with a snug band at the cuff. The top was loose and hung nicely and gathered right around the hips turning into a tight little mini skirt. If you were around in the 80s you can appreciate this style, if not, trust me, it was in style back then.

My legs were my best feature and I took every opportunity to show them off. The great thing about this skirt was that with the gathering around the hips, I can always pull the dress up or down depending on whether I was at home and school under the watchful eyes of my dad and the nuns of Holy Family, or around the boys from my brother's high school. I looked great and felt wonderful. I added dangling earrings to the look and made sure my curly hair softly fell on my shoulders. As a freshman in high school, this was a big deal for me, my coming out party announcing that I was now grown up. I had my matching high-heels and I felt very sexy and beautiful. I was no longer in elementary school and was a grown sophisticated woman now.

School that day was uneventful. Every other girl had the same idea, a chance to dress up in their best outfits and show off their style. I took my photos and was now on my way to meet my brother at the neighboring boys' school. I usually went home with my best friend Helen but for some reason she was out that day. I was on my own which didn't happen very often. We went everywhere together, navigating the bus ride to and from school and hanging out after school until our parents came home. She was my wing-woman, I was hers, and we watched out for each other. This particular day, I was alone and had to navigate getting to my brother's school all by myself. I didn't mind as it was another sign of my independence. I felt very powerful and at 13, knew I was finally stepping into my own.

I boarded the city bus in front of my school with at least a dozen other school girls and took the 15 minute ride to my brother's. After crossing underneath the 2 Freeway on San Fernando Road, the bus settled at my exit. As I said goodbye to my friends on the bus and disembarked alone, I began walking, school bag in hand towards the busy intersection I had to cross. I was feeling very independent and pretty, walking down the street with my beautiful white dress and my little heals. My brother's school was on San Fernando Road at the opposite end of a busy, large 6 lane road. I had to back track a really long city block under the freeway overpass and cross at the signal at the end of the street to get to him. There were railroad tracks and nothing else on my side of the road and his school was on the other side.

Not one minute passed when three scary looking men in a beat up car started hooting and hollering at me. I was painfully aware at that moment that I was all alone and had no defense against anyone wishing to do me harm. I began to quicken my pace and avert my eyes from any cars passing by. Luckily they drove past without incident.

A few minutes later I heard another round of whistling and noises headed in my direction. Another car was slowly heading my way carrying a group of four men. I heard a loud whistle, rounds of ooh baby baby, come over here, and obnoxious smacks of kisses coming my way. It wasn't the ideal male attention I was looking for. It was really disgusting, scary and something I had never experienced before. These men were older and not anywhere near high school age, so in my mind, it couldn't be easily blown off. This was a real threat to me. I was scared, terrified and thoughts of all the warnings I'd received over my lifetime raced through my mind. I was told over and over not to be anywhere alone or risk getting kidnapped and raped. All the stuff 13 years olds are warned about came racing through my mind.

I felt dirty and terrified, thought I would be hurt and ashamed that I was being taken for a prostitute. The Catholic guilt over causing something so dreadful flooded over me. I kept pulling down my skirt as low as it would go and stared straight at my destination, heart racing and panic ensuing. I was scared, all alone and didn't know what to do but to walk even faster. Running would draw too much attention. They kept yelling as their car came closer to me. I glanced around quickly, praying for someone to help me, a friendly hero to save me, but there was no one in sight. My only protection was my backpack. I took my bag and I put it in front of me, clutching it tighter covering my chest vacillating between feeling fear and beating myself up for dressing this way, for putting myself in this situation asking for male attention. I felt my energy shrink. I continued berating myself. I was responsible for this, I asked for this because here I was wearing a slutty outfit looking like a prostitute. I avoided eye contact, and tried to ignore them.

Finally, they drove past me and left, distant sounds of catcalls. I finally reached my destination and all the confidence of feeling sexy and beautiful was drained completely out of me. I now felt cheap and ugly, only good enough to draw attention from perverts wishing to prey on cheap girls who dared flaunt their assets in public.

From that point on, I was on a mission to hide any semblance of sexuality I had. I played small, dressed conservatively, purposefully carried myself in a manner that would not draw attention to me as a woman. And the best defense, I put on 100 pounds to make sure no man would be attracted to me. I packed on the weight to make myself undesirable so that men wouldn't want to violate me. I learned to walk tall, looking straight ahead, powerful body language to show any possible threat that I was not one to deal with. I worked at trying to prove that I was not a potential victim and was by no means vulnerable.

I walked like a man and turned down my sexuality. It was dirty, it can hurt you, you only get what you ask for and it was all your fault. Unfortunately, I blamed myself for what these gross perverted men who like to prey on little girls did and I turned down my light and my beauty. I stopped flirting, I stopped dressing sexy and seductively, I stopped attempting to draw guys' approving glances and I sought to go back to being invisible. I became more guarded in my friendships with guys, in my interactions with men, no longer carelessly showcasing my assets, and no longer spent my free time cavorting and socializing with guys.

I became a buddy, one of the guys, I was safer that way. I can be seen as one of them without being vulnerable or exposing myself to harm. I did have guy friends, but they were not the flirting, tickling, teasing kinds of friendships. When I was interested in someone, I became more aloof so as not to attract negative attention from them. Thus, they never knew I was interested.

That experience at 13 years old left such an indelible mark on me and my sexuality. That day, I closed down my sexual energy so much and never opened it up until years later when I started doing this work. Going into my marriage shutting this part of who I am affected me and our relationship. I didn't always enjoy sex. I still liked clothes but always chose something more conservative, more sensible. I no longer enjoyed the feeling of dressing up and the feel of clothes on my body. I never wanted to dress in a sexy manner and was scared of anything that was a little revealing.

HEALING FROM SEXUAL ABUSE

Often times, when we've been hurt or violated or mistreated in some way, we revert to being invisible, which is the polar opposite of what the Playmate desires. She wants to be center stage, she is always put together and loves to watch heads spin as she struts by. However, because most of us have never been taught to protect this beautiful part of us with the CEO, we become vulnerable being the beautiful sexy goddess that we are. Just as wearing a rolex in an undesirable neighbourhood would make you susceptible to robbery, a woman can become prey. Most women respond to this fear by not wanting to show up, by hiding or becoming invisible in an effort to remain safe.

I remember when I was a little girl, I loved going into my mom's closet. I would wear her heels, the gorgeous wraps and red lipstick. I was walking around like I was a little princess, and I wanted everybody to see me and tell me how adorable I looked. Little girls love playing dress up. They love dressing and feeling beautiful and will flaunt it around to any audience they can find. There's a point, however, when we are growing up that we are made wrong to want to flaunt our beauty. This part of us gets cut off because we are either invalidated, someone tells us the lipstick we got all over our face is a mess, or we're told to be modest, not show off our bodies otherwise we become labelled as promiscuous. We are taught to cover up. We are told not to be conceited, that it's wrong to have a desire for attention. All of a sudden we don't feel safe by being in touch with our bodies or being in touch with our sensuality and sexuality.

THE NOT SO PERFECT COMBINATION

By the way, the Playmate energy combined with the Mother energy is a perfect combination for prey. She is the woman that is beautiful and sexy while also being sweet and nurturing. She is very mothering, concerned with being nice and giving in, rather than taking care of her own needs. That was me, I wanted to be beautiful yet was taught to always be nice which meant accept whatever someone was dishing out. This also made me very giving as well as compliant with men. This woman often gets taken advantage of by men. This made me and anyone with this combination very vulnerable to predators. Playmate-Mothers are usually sexually active at a young age. They want to please the boys they are with, wanting to make them happy and of course their connection to beauty, naturally opens them up to early sexual exploration. That might have been me had I not turned down my sexuality at 13 and of course, had I not been so innocent.

SEXUAL HEALING

Sexual energy contains within it powerful creative energy. When we shut down or tone down our sexual energy, we actually tone down our creativity and our ability to bring forth life to anything; a project, a book, a business or a baby. This blocks our creative capacity in a relationship or business, anything we are attempting to bring forth. We can turn the dial up on our sexual energy when we are about to make love to our husbands or we are flirting with somebody. That has the effect of increasing the chemistry between us. But when I am walking down a dark alleyway, I am going to turn that sucker off because I do not want to be exuding any attractive sexual energy and become prey to a predator.

Healing our sexual energy, our sensuality and our ability to love and live in our bodies can open us up to exquisite new experiences in the world. There are many ways to heal past hurt and of course if you have experienced any sexual trauma, please seek out a professional to guide you toward true and everlasting freedom from the binds of past abuse. Here, I offer you one powerful healing technique. In this next exercise, we are going to look at where in your life you shut off or toned down your sexuality. There may be lots of experiences that have had a negative effect on how you can show up to the world. We are going to find that first experience that had the most significant impact on you, that first experience that cut you off from your body, from your senses, from your own sensuality and sexuality. We are looking for an experience that impacted how beautiful and sexy you can allow yourself to get in touch with and to feel.

Once we find that time and experience that had a negative effect on how you interact in your world in regards to your sexuality, we're going to heal it and release its emotional charge. This will free up your ability and willingness to be sensual and sexy while allowing your CEO to take care of keeping you safe (we'll address how the CEO keeps you safe later). You no longer have to hide underneath all the baggy clothes, baseball cap or excess weight. Some examples of the first instance of toning down your sexuality can be conscious or unconscious. Children naturally want to discover every inch of their beautiful bodies. They touch their bodies and play with themselves and so many times are invalidated for their innocent exploration. That could be one point where you might find you were cut off from your body. It could also be some form of sexual abuse or violation.

I want you to find some experience that had the biggest impact for you. All of this happened to me on an unconscious level. I had no idea I was doing this to myself until years later. When I realized I made myself invisible, that I closed down my sexual energy, my ability to be sensual, I decided it was now up to me to reintegrate that part of me with more control so that I can feel safe. I recruited the help of my CEO. As the warrior, she taught me how to set boundaries, she taught me how to stay safe and she protected me when I needed her. She is also in control of that little knob that says I'm on a date with a man I really like, turn up the sexual energy or I'm walking down a dark alley in the middle the night, sexual energy down. You have that ability to be in control so you can show up and still be beautiful and still be sexy and still be vibrant and alive all the while, you are protected, and are no longer prey.

EXERCISE

In this healing meditation, we are going to look at where we closed down our sexual energy and cut ourselves off from our body and how the CEO can set those boundaries to protect you.

MEDITATION TO RELEASE SEXUAL ABUSE

Sit comfortably in a chair and take a long deep cleansing breath. Put your feet flat on the ground and take another deep breath. Say hello to your grounding cord, release it if you still have one hooked in and create a new one. Attach that grounding cord from the base of your spine and watch it go all the way down into the center of the planet. Give it a nice little tug. Make sure it is connected and releasing all the energy you're ready to let go of today.

This is a great time to validate your body by giving your full attention to it. We neglect our body so much as we drag it throughout our day and we forget to thank it for its support, strength, and cooperation to allow us to get through the day and accomplish all we want and need. Thank your body, send it love, validate it for its strength and vitality.

Create a line, a timeline out in front of you, a line that starts from birth up to your current age. Notice marks on that timeline that divide it into increments of decades, every 10 years or increments of five years if you are younger than 30. Allow a purple dot to appear at every age where you might have been invalidated for your sexuality or have been victimized sexually.

Maybe you had a circumstance or an event where you decided on a conscious level or maybe even an unconscious level to close down your ability to truly enjoy life and be in touch with your body. Perhaps you were told it was wrong to experience full joy of your senses, to be sensual, to relish in the sights, smells, tastes and feel of the world around you. You may have been yelled at for touching yourself as a child. Maybe there was a time where you were made wrong to flirt, when you were simply being friendly and open. Perhaps as a child you were reprimanded for talking to a stranger or told not to be so trusting and unguarded. You might have been touched in a way that made you feel uncomfortable. If there were any times you were sexually violated, abused or harmed in any way, allow that to light up.

Allow purple dots to pop up on that timeline for every one of these points. Trust that all the purple dots will light up, whether or not you have conscious memory or recollection of specific events. Now take a rose and starting from birth, from that beginning point, run it along that line out in front of you. Just like a vacuum hose, watch that rose suck up all those purple points along that timeline, all the way up to your current age. After you are done, take that rose about 2 feet out in front of you, put a firecracker under it and blow that up.

Create a big golden sun above your head and start to call back your energy. Call back your energy from anyone and everyone who may have violated you. Call back your energy from anyone you are still holding onto hurt and resentment from unwanted advances. Call back your energy from every place you left it, where you decided it was not okay to be sexual, to enjoy your senses, or to be in touch with your physical body. Call back your energy from anywhere you decided to turn down your ability to enjoy life, laugh, feel joyous and be full of bliss. Once that sun is full of your own energy, begin to bring your own beautiful vibration down to fill in your body and your aura, the space around your body.

Notice how you feel now that you've released all the old limitations to your beauty, your sensuality and your sexuality easily and effortlessly. Take some time to journal, not what you released, but who you are now that you have let go of all of these stifling pictures.

Seventeen

LET HER OUT TO PLAY

"Laughter is timeless, imagination has no age, and dreams are forever. Let your inner child come out to play with the playful energy of the Playmate."

SEXY TIME

No doubt about it, the Playmate is responsible for her sex appeal and bringing her sexy on. Sex, sensual and sexual energy is an essential part of ourselves. It is natural. We are the sexy force on this planet and it's time we own it. When we shut that down or when it starts to dry up, we lose touch with parts of ourselves. Once healed, having sex and great orgasms can bring pleasure and bliss. Women who have regular sex are healthier, live longer and attract more wealth than women who have sporadic or non-existent sex.

I am not going to advocate going out and having wild passionate sex with just anyone, but if you are in a romantic sexual safe relationship, bring it on. Sex brings life force to a relationship. Passion ignites the sparks and creates a dynamic bond between two people, deeper than friendships or other platonic relationships. I believe sex is the ultimate gift given to us by the Universe to encourage procreation, keeping life alive and maintaining our own existence. It's a great feeling that releases dopamine and oxytocin, giving you the energy you need to go out and make things happen in the world.

Sex and pleasure is healing for us as women and allows us to tap into our creative energy. Sexual energy is creative energy. It gives us more power and more energy. Creating fun, sexual tension with a man is for You. It is creating pleasure in you. You show up as a sexual, beautiful, sexy, playmate for you, to tap into your pleasure centers. When you are able to tap into your own pleasure, the man will feed off that. That is what entices him. And when you hold a man sexually, you own him. You have so much power over a man. Not in a manipulative way, but igniting that instinctive desire and distinct connection between a man and a woman. In a relationship, all it takes is a look that says “I want you”, wearing something that makes you feel sexy, or thinking sexy, juicy thoughts while looking at your partner. For those times when you are not in a sexual relationship, you can create sensual experiences for yourself by luxuriating in your five senses. Slow down and taste an incredible meal, put on some luxurious lotion, wear perfume that brings a smile to your face and listen to soothing, soul filling music you love. Whatever you choose, be intentional, slow down and breathe it all in and experience the bliss available to you.

PROTECTING THE PLAYMATE

The reason A-list actresses can stand on the red carpet looking stunning in clothes and jewelry worth hundreds of thousands of dollars is that they have body guards. No one can get within 100 feet of them without permission, which gives them the room and freedom to simply be stunning and gorgeous while remaining safe. If you can imagine a situation in which there were no bodyguards, a mob would attack them and they would have to recoil in fear or defend themselves. Not a pretty sight. We see this all the time in the news when actors and actresses have to duck their heads, look down, run and recoil as they rush through a mob of photographers while out to dinner or walking their dog, trying to evade their imposing presence. A much different picture than the serene poised look on the red carpet. As you will learn later in this book, the CEO acts like a bodyguard to the Playmate. The CEO makes sure she is protected, is ready to act and pulls her out of danger so that the Playmate can remain poised and look stunning.

PLAYMATE CONCLUSION

The Playmate is all about having fun, enjoying life and all the senses, connecting with people, places and things with passion. She looks and feels great and creates beautiful surroundings. This is a woman's masculine energy because her focus is on the outer world and on an elemental level, the air connects her to herself. Air cannot be contained. She is the wild child, the free, spontaneous, flowing and unrestrained Self. Air or wind connects your spirit to your body.

The playmate is able to connect with and lift up the spirits of people around her. She has fun, enjoys life, sings out loud, and dances. She loves her body and everything sensual; enticing aromas, incredible food, the feel of beautiful silk or cashmere against her skin and anything soft and luxurious. The primary desire of a playmate is to look and feel fabulous, to enjoy the pleasures and to have fun.

Ways to get in touch with your Inner Playmate

- Feel the wind on your face or the warm or cool air against your skin
- Get dirty, wet, messy and enjoy being a kid again
- Dress up for a night out or even a night in
- Wear sexy lingerie
- Participate in something that makes you laugh out loud
- Practice eating slowly and tasting each bite.

PART IV

The Bad*ss CEO

Eighteen

THE CEO

"A woman who knows her worth and follows her dreams is a force to be reckoned with. She doesn't need to announce her power, it speaks for itself."

WHO IS THE CEO?

The next Feminine archetype that validates us as women today is the CEO. Unless you have been living under a rock, you are probably most familiar with the CEO. The CEO in us is the warrior, the badass, the woman that gets up every day with a plan and accomplishes all that she sets out to do. She is the woman who shows up at work or place of business, running the business or project. She is in charge and does it well. She can manage people, projects and her entire to-do list. She follows through consistently and is responsible for the financial success and status in her life. She is the woman that is strong and powerful and makes things happen in her life.

This is the mental aspect of a woman, the part responsible for the mind, the thinking, the judgement, the logic and the reasoning. She says what she does and does what she says. She is clear on her boundaries and assures that her boundaries are respected. The CEO knows when and how to say No and stands guard at the portal of all her decisions and experiences in life. She can run a household like clockwork and assures that she is respected, listened to and doesn't get run over by her children, husband, co-workers or other significant relationships.

The CEO is practical, grounded and wise. She knows what she wants and how to get things done. In fact, she follows through with her plans in a way that can leave most people marveling at her steadfastness and straightforwardness. This is not a woman who wears her heart on her sleeve like the Mother, rather, she knows that if she wants something, she needs to roll up her sleeves and put in the work required to get it. She is responsible for prosperity. If you are finding that wealth, resources, and all the things you need to accomplish what you need to do are not coming into your life, this is an indication that the CEO is out of balance.

The CEO is all about organization. The CEO is about achievement and accomplishment. The CEO is about making things happen and getting things done. The CEO is organized, never cluttered, and she knows where to find everything she needs, refusing to waste time searching for papers beneath piles of junk on her desk. Everyone knows that she will get the job done. If she commits to a task, you can rest assured that it will be accomplished in a timely manner, if not sooner. And you can bet it will be done right the first time. Her word is law. She doesn't commit unless she knows she can follow through and is honest about herself and her achievements.

WHY I LOVE THE CEO?

Owning the CEO aspect in our lives means stepping into that powerful warrior of a woman. This is the energy that allows us to powerfully step into our feminine because the CEO is what protects us. The CEO is what makes sure that we are safe. The CEO allows us to function successfully in a physical, tangible and materialistic world. The CEO is what keeps us from over-giving, keeps us balanced and keeps us from getting taken advantage of. When the CEO does her job, it allows us to have more fun, to play more, to create more success and fully step into our feminine energy.

BOUNDARIES

The CEO sets boundaries. She is clear on her boundary line and doesn't allow anyone to cross it or cross her. She is responsible for maintaining respect, self respect and respect from others. She assures that she is respected in her home and in her work. She assures that she is listened to. She doesn't get run over by her children. She doesn't get taken advantage of by her husband. She doesn't allow herself to feel depleted or empty. She knows what and where those lines are and she clearly communicates them with others. The CEO has both foresight and hindsight.

The CEO has enough foresight to consider possible scenarios and knows what she will and will not allow in her experience. She knows when and how to say No and she is very clear about her No. She is not wishy-washy and does not allow anyone or anything to change her mind unless she has new information or a clear self honoring intention. She stands sentineled, protecting all her decisions and experiences in life. She is in charge. She is in control. She knows what she is doing and why she is doing it.

Of course, for some of us, boundaries have to be tested to be set. Life has a beautiful way of providing opportunities for growth, for learning what works and what doesn't work for us, what feels good and what doesn't feel good. Oftentimes we have to learn through mistakes, mis-steps or past experiences. We can also learn from the experiences of others, watching others deal with certain situations, from the media, social and traditional, and even from stories as they unfold in literature and movies we watch. In these instances, in walks the High Priestess. The High Priestess is present through all of life's ups and downs. She is so connected with herself and her internal experience that she clearly knows what is okay and what is not okay, what feels good and what does not feel good to her. The CEO listens to this part of her and steps in to take action. She says next time this is not going to happen and takes appropriate action.

POWER OF SAYING NO

So many times as women, we wait until we are fed up, we've been pushed to the limit and have nothing left before we say No. The Mother says Yes, the Mother gives others what they want and need, and the Mother goes out of her way to put others' needs before her own. The High Priestess connects you with your truth, your true answer. When you are in touch with her, you know when to say Yes and you know when to say No without compromising your needs, your desires, or your spirit. Because most women are still programmed to lead with the motherly role, most women are quick to say yes, to give in, to provide everyone with their needs before checking on how it will affect them.

The CEO assures that your yeses mean yes and your no's mean no. The CEO can say Yes when she is clear on her decision to follow through without any self-sacrifice and she says No, maintaining her boundaries without feeling any guilt. She never waits until she is fed up or depleted before she puts her foot down.

I'm sure you've observed the all too familiar dreaded child-parent interaction. The child asks for a toy in a store. Mom says No, usually her first reaction. The child proceeds to throw a tantrum, begins to plead, cry, scream or whine. After being pushed to her limit and in an attempt to quiet the child and avoid uncomfortable stares from judging eyes, the mother goes back on her word and gives in to the child. I cringe when I see this because I know how this story eventually unfolds. The child's tolerance level for the "No" increases, it doesn't mean much to them and in fact it means that the next time they hear "No", they simply need to "turn up" their fight. If the first scenario took three minutes of kicking and screaming, the next time the child is told No or doesn't get her way, she will fight for at least that long and go on a little longer. She will even step up her tantrum, making it last longer and louder.

I know it can be difficult, believe me I've been there. I have been on the other end of the judgemental stares at the grocery store as I try to stand my ground with my son. Sometimes our first reaction sets us up for failure if we do in fact want to rethink our initial response. Growing up, I heard "because I said so" quite a bit. Whenever I asked for something and my father said No, I would ask why and all I received back was "because I said so". The feeling of being utterly dismissed, not being able to negotiate and feel heard made me feel bad about myself and put a wedge between me and my relationship with my father. I hated it. I felt he didn't care about me, that I didn't matter and that he was just being a plain old jerk.

I knew growing up that when I had my own kids, I didn't want to be the "No" mom. I made a conscious decision with my son to not overuse the word "No". At the same time, I needed to affirm my rules and boundaries. I wanted him to feel heard and to be able to stand up for himself. I wanted him to learn cooperation, respect and communication. I encouraged him to share with me reasons he felt I should say Yes. When he asked for something, my immediate response was never No, but rather “maybe”, “let me think about it” or “is there a reason I should say Yes when I want to say No?”. I needed a way out, a way to change my mind while not compromising my authority.

I told him that he needed to convince me and give me reasons why he wanted to buy a toy or skip dinner to play with his friends. Initially, I created a monster. What I created was a relentless lawyer who got really good at negotiating. He would go on and on about his case and happily took on the challenge of convincing me. Needless to say, there were many times I felt my frustration build up inside of me. Underneath the surface, this was just the same as saying No. I had to adjust my strategy and decided that instead of saying No, if I heard enough and decided not to give in, I would say “the negotiation is over”. That was my code for “No”.

In the beginning, he didn’t understand what I meant but when I kept repeating it and he learned I was not going to back down, he realized that when I said “the negotiation is over”, that meant that there was no convincing, he was not getting his way and to let it go. Meanwhile, he got his air time and felt respected and heard. And he knew I was the boss. After a few tests, we rarely had an argument, had great communication and were able to respect each other.

Some children tend to shut down when they hear “No”. They feel defeated. Hearing No often can lead to a defeatist attitude, expressing itself later in life as the habit of always giving up before they even try to achieve something. Saying “No” if it must be used, can be softened by bringing in the compassionate Mother or the loving High priestess or even the playful Playmate. I remember when I was young my parents were very overprotective of me. As a young girl, I was never allowed to just hang out in the neighbourhood. We didn’t live in a very good neighbourhood to begin with and they wanted to keep a close eye on me to make sure I was safe. Of course as a young girl, it was a source of contention. Her game of singing "no going outside" as she tickled me made the entire interaction about connecting with my mom, receiving love and having fun. Now looking back, all I remember is my mother connecting with me and me asking for her to tickle me by singing "I want to go outside". I didn't feel denied, I didn't feel upset, all I felt was love and playfulness. And of course, my mom was able to connect with me and not have to deal with a tantrum.

OWN YOUR NO

The CEO exudes confidence and unapologetically prioritizes herself, her life, and her needs. She wields immense power when it comes to saying No and fully embraces this power. Every Yes requires a No to something else, and the CEO makes these choices consciously. To lead effectively, she must learn to honor her needs, desires, and values, and this often requires saying No to distractions, others' needs, and affairs that don't align with her inner Queen, the High Priestess, and her higher vision.

Once you say No, going back on it means you're not honoring your word, and it may make others less likely to honor your word in the future. The High Priestess allows you as a woman to get in touch with what is right in the moment. If for some reason, you are not in touch, it's okay to say "let me think about it or I'm not sure right now, I need some time". In fact, leaving your answer open until you've had time to decide is a wise choice. The CEO is also able to take her time to gather the information she needs to make a decision. But once a decision is made, you must be willing to stand by it. If you are intentional with your answer, then others will respect your word. For some women who have been trained into being nice or subservient, No can be difficult. Sometimes we have to act like we own the "No" until it becomes comfortable. The people around us, just like us, need a little training. This may be new to many women who are used to taking care of others and making sure everyone's needs are met before their own.

I personally don't think I use the specific word "No" a lot, which can sometimes be harsh, but I'm working on owning my "No". When you own your "No", then you can allow the other archetypes to assist you in communicating it in a gentle, respectful, beautiful, fun way. When you assert your boundaries, most people will be okay with it, especially if you are compassionate, empathetic and if appropriate, even a little playful. I've averted lots of mother-son fights by lovingly owning my "No".

As you begin to take on the challenge of stepping into your CEO, you may need to remove the smile and present a stern demeanor, at least initially. If you've been running your Mother energy all along giving in to everything, people may not believe you when you stand up for yourself. I know many women who begin to honor themselves and inadvertently upset or disappoint others. That's okay, some people don't like it when you set boundaries, especially when they've been able to walk all over you in the past. Taking away the smile or putting on a serious face will help your case until you can balance your energies and are able to say No with a soft edge.

Once you are feeling more balanced, then you can step back and say No gently with a qualifier such as "It doesn't make sense to me right now" or "It's not a priority at the moment for me". Until then, no explanation is necessary and can in fact weaken your answer. If you do it with a smile and with genuine compassion, others will respect your decision and will respect you. When you respect your boundaries, other people will respect your boundaries as well.

The CEO is unapologetic when setting and holding her boundary. When she wants something or when she says what is happening right now is not okay with her, she does not make apologies for her decision. Women are notorious for constantly saying sorry. Unless you have done something maliciously to someone else, remove that word completely from your vocabulary. That was something that I had to work on myself. When I had to send my regrets or say No, I would precede emails, texts, phone calls with, “I'm really sorry but . . .”. Even in the midst of a conversation I would continue to say, “I'm sorry”. A male friend of mine asked if I had some information he was interested in and I replied, I’m sorry I don’t. He stopped me and said stop saying sorry. Apparently he had heard it come out of my mouth one too many times.

I started to pay attention to how often I apologize. It did come out of my mouth often. I also started to pay attention to conversations with men. I quickly noticed they never apologized. When they said No, there seemed to be a period after it. Whereas my conversations seemed to flow more like . . . I’m sorry, I can’t go to your party, I’m sorry I’m busy with a big work project, I’m sorry the restaurant was out of what you wanted or I’m sorry the concert was sold out. They simply said I can’t or I don’t want to or just plain old No. They offered no apologies or qualifiers for their decision. Their response was simply a statement. As women, we need to learn how to be unapologetically grounded in what we want. And that takes confidence, being clear and owning your No.

Nineteen

POWER

"A woman is like a tea bag - you can't tell how strong she is until you put her in hot water."

~ Eleanor Roosevelt ~

THE PHANTOM

If anyone knows me well, they know I am obsessed with musical theatre. I was talking about a great musical "Phantom of the Opera" with a male friend of mine who happened to enjoy seeing Broadway shows. Even though I thoroughly enjoyed Phantom, it wasn't one of my favorites but I found myself telling him that he will absolutely love it. I was surprised by my initial comment and spent time pondering my praise for the musical. In fact, over my adult life, I have had to plead with and coerce many a man to accompany me to a musical. I have learned that watching men in tights sing and prance around the stage was not exactly the highlight of most men's weekends. Nevertheless, because they were in the process of wooing me, they politely obliged to accompany me to one of my favorite pastimes.

There were several shows I took these men to and although most managed to stay awake during the entire performance, when asked what they thought, most of the time, they simply stated "interesting" and after noticing a disappointed look on my face, clarified their review with "it was good". In contrast however, anytime I suggested a date to see Phantom of the Opera, they left the theatre impressed, an excited look on their face and many a man has expressed that this was the first time they have seen a musical and really enjoyed it. They were interested in seeing others in the future.

I pondered this stark contrasting viewpoint seemingly based on a different title and initially chalked it off as a liking of the dark story line or the fact that there were no men in tutus prancing around stage. When I offered my friend my firm recommendation, I started to contemplate more, asking myself "What is it about Phantom were men drawn to?" After all, this was nothing more than a story of a dark, hurt and bitter man who was rejected after trying to hypnotize a beautiful woman of light into his dark cave where he can have her for himself and strip her of her own life. And then it hit me. The reason they liked it was because it was a story about a dark, hurt and bitter man who was rejected trying to hypnotize a beautiful woman of light into his dark cave where he can have her all to himself and strip her of her own life.

A relationship expert and good friend Carol Allen says that a man's burden is rejection while the woman's burden is waiting. In the traditional male-female dance, men put themselves out there, initiating contact with a woman, wooing and pursuing her and asking for her hand for a lifetime. A woman on the other hand, has to wait, wait until the man is ready and wait for him to decide to choose her.

Follow me with this analogy. I'm not saying all men are dark but what I am saying is that there are certain men who see a prize, a woman they want all to themselves, who will save them from their own darkness. He is unable to see his own light and in this fear, he hides beneath the shadows, he puts on a show, an act, a mask, to get what he wants without risking being vulnerable. These men have low self esteem, or have been beaten by life, and could not even fathom a woman coming to him on her own will, choosing to forsake all others for him. Afterall, he is scared of what she will find underneath his exterior mask. In this simple belief, he has already failed. But in his endurance, he begins to play a game, a pursuit full of charm, magnetism, coercion, threats and desperate attempts to lure her into his cave. Once there, he plays on her fears, strips her of her own esteem and reminds her that she is nothing without him. She begins to doubt herself, wonders what it will be like to be with him, feels as if she owes him something or worse, feels she is strong enough to save him from his misery. She sees the good inside of him and wants to know more. In one climactic scene, she lifts up his veil, looks at him behind the mask he wears wanting to see the beauty within. For a moment, he allows it but then his fear turns to anger, which turns to rage and then to hate and he lashes out at her. In the end, she rejects him and he never fully recovers. Heed this warning, protect your heart and know that you cannot save this man from himself, no matter how much love you have to give.

MAINTAINING INDEPENDENCE FROM MEN

When I was in my 30's I had a boyfriend who said he couldn't understand why people in relationships spent so much time apart. He talked about couples that do their "own thing" as a negative. He wanted someone he can spend time with, enjoying things together and doing normal day to day chores with; grocery shopping, running errands, etc. I thought I had died and gone to heaven. I scored a man who actually wanted to spend all his time with me. I followed him around in life. I watched what he wanted to watch, went to the games he wanted to see, and ate at the restaurants he wanted to eat at.

Eventually, I found out he was just like any other guy. He got claustrophobic and started looking for that exit sign, a little breathing room. I took it completely personally. He lied to me even though he never came right out to say it. I started to conclude that he didn't really like me and didn't desire to spend every waking and sleeping hour with me.

I was resentful that he had not chosen to spend every waking moment with me but honestly, revelled in the time he was gone. Oh, don't get me wrong, I complained. I was disappointed when he had to work long hours or when he wanted to go to the gym without me. I waited around for him day in and day out. There were those days, however, when I knew he was going to be gone for a while. I mean, not just late, but gone for the evening. I secretly looked forward to those days. If I truly knew he wasn't just getting away from me, I would resign to planning my day or night without him. I'd make a facial or massage appointment. I would light the fire and read quietly on my comfortable sofa that envelopes you, which had been hijacked for his sole purpose of watching sports. I would light candles, catch up with my girlfriends and laugh with my son. I would plan a night out or do something I loved doing, something that I had neglected for so long. It was so rejuvenating and filled me with a sense of joy and peace. It was the only time I was able to reconnect with me, with who I am and with my interests.

One day we had a blow out. I was frustrated that I was losing who I was. I no longer laughed as much as I used to, socialized as much as I did, nor engaged in the activities that filled my soul and passion. It was his fault because he didn't share these interests with me nor did he find them very enticing. He always said, "go do them". What he didn't realize was that if I did, it would take away from our time together. I would be too busy to be with him and I didn't want to risk losing even more precious time with him. I wanted him to help me to be more of me. I wanted him to care about the things I cared about and to be excited about the things I wanted him to be excited about. Well, he made it clear that unless I was excited about them, he couldn't be. I wanted him on board but he made me realize that I hadn't even gotten on board. I had to do what I love and not wait for permission. It wasn't his fault, I chose to let go of my interests and my desires.

I began to get back in touch with my passions. I read, I cooked, I looked into volunteering and I signed up to run a marathon. I reconnected with my friends and reinvigorated my social life. I was finally okay being me and letting him be him. I was even okay with him doing his own thing. I didn't frown when he said he wanted to go get a hair cut on our only weekend together. I gave him a kiss goodbye, let him go and went on to take care of some things I had been neglecting.

PROTECT YOUR HEART

The Mother knows how to love unconditionally. The High Priestess sees the good in everyone and the Playmate knows how to make herself desirable. I believe the world needs a little more of this combination of acceptance, this unconditional love, this ability to see through the mask people wear because of their own fears. At the same time, a woman can lose herself in a game she has no business playing if she is not careful. A woman in love will give everything to her man. She requires the CEO to be smart with her heart, to get to know a man before she gives him everything and to be ready to walk away when boundaries are crossed. She gives him a chance, is constantly paying attention to her needs, her desires and her emotional barometer and communicates immediately when things are off for her. She knows her limits, knows what she will and will not tolerate and is willing to take immediate action to preserve her body, her emotions, and her soul.

YOUR LEGAL TEAM

There is great virtue in doing the right thing and being open, honest and full of integrity. I believe in karma and fighting battles is not for the feminine. It is not what she is designed to do. That being said, there are times when you will have to stand up for yourself or some wrong doing. You may not want to get in the ring and get dirty (very unlady like) but you will have to make decisions that are tough and gather a team to come to your aid or defense. This team gives you the power you require to move forward. Maybe you were taken advantage of, maybe you lost a partnership or found yourself stuck in an unscrupulous agreement. The CEO's job is to gather a support team, experts in their particular field. This includes legal help.

Many of my clients and followers are on a spiritual path. They live their lives with a sense of self-consciousness, self-awareness, and taking 100% responsibility for their actions. Because we live at cause, we expect positive things to happen. There is a dangerous drawback that often occurs for positive loving women (think Mother and High Priestess) who are into personal development, were sold into the law of attraction and perhaps have a metaphysical approach to their thinking. Many buy into the whole "I'm just going to think positively" mentality. They think bad things are not going to happen to them. This optimism bias is not in and of itself a bad thing. It is nice to live life thinking that good things will happen to us. This is how the High Priestess lives. This keeps us focused on the positive, relieving stress and tension in daily decision making, and moves us toward people, resources and places that will support our positive mindset and create beneficial results. By acknowledging that we have this optimism bias and being aware of how it affects us, we can make better decisions and avoid potential pitfalls that can be disastrous.

While it is admirable to go about your day thinking everything will work itself out to your benefit, the reality is we live in a physical world and in this physical world, things happen. People take advantage of other people, there are people who don't follow through on contracts, and there are others who have ill intent. Having safeguards against this type of injustice is the smart way a CEO woman runs her life. She has iron clad contracts signed before going into deals. She carries the proper insurance to cover her assets. Her assets are in legal entities that protect her and her family, she has the best financial support she can afford, and she seeks legal counsel when required. She gathers experts who can advise her on not only what is ethically right, but also on her legal rights. Knowing your rights is equally important. I now have a legal team in place and anytime I have a legal question, I call up and consult with an expert in the area of question. I never sign a contract without having them review it.

One of the biggest mistakes I made was walking away from my marriage with nothing. We had a very successful business we were running together and at the time, the business was the only source of my income. I had just given birth to my son and I was going through a divorce. Although, I still believe I made the best decision I could have made at the time knowing what I knew, it took me seven tough years to finally get back on my feet. I was beginning my spiritual journey at the time and because of the ugly conditions surrounding my relationship and the business we ran together, I just wanted out. I wanted to take what I believed was the high road. I didn’t want to fight, didn’t want to drag my son through the court system and didn’t want to participate in any battle over who gets what. I lost quite a bit in my divorce and some very close friends of mine did as well because we didn't fight for our rights. We didn't reach out to people that knew the law or people that could help us protect ourselves, we only backed off the bullying and threats that came from the other side.

We went through a paralegal and signed the divorce paperwork severing the marriage with little negotiation. In my heart, I knew I could rebuild and I knew I could create a beautiful life for myself. However, I was naïve about the amount of time and energy it would take me to re-establish a foundation for me and my baby. I had the right intention but was too naïve to understand the repercussions. It wasn't all or nothing, there was another way.

Having guided clients through similar proceedings, I had an entirely different perspective I could offer them. All of my clients are beautiful people who have high morals and standards and understand that life is what you make of it. They understand that surrounding yourself with positive people, positive intentions and positive thinking will bring about positive results. When faced with tough issues I gave them the same counsel I am giving you here. Remain in your positive emotional state and mindset and have a powerful team around you that will fight the fight alongside you. As women, we think we have to do it ourselves, that we have to figure it out ourselves. The CEO 100% knows she cannot do it on her own. She's the one that is always making sure that she seeks the help she requires.

There are wonderful people who will stand up for what is right. To them, it is not a fight, they are not getting pulled down into a spiral of negativity. They are doing what they believe is right. These include attorneys, lawyers, advocates, field experts, mediators and consultants who love what they do and love these types of negotiations, proceedings and trials. They are very good at what they do and don't get emotionally involved.

As women, we are often willing to give up our rights, to succumb to other people's needs and to acquiesce to other people's desires. Having expert assistance allows us to stand up for ourselves without getting into the ring, getting dirty and fighting the fight. Don't get me wrong, the CEO knows she can get down and dirty if need be, but the smart CEO makes sure she never has to. She lets the lawyers, the accountants or whomever that professional person is, take care of it all. You could just continue to show up in your beauty and in your grace knowing that you are protected by experts whose job it is to assure that you are getting treated fairly.

It is part of our Feminine energy, the High Priestess, to hold the light and the space for everything to work out well. The CEO partners with her and affirms that yes, everything will work out, but we are going to make sure that we are covered and protected in case life does happen. It's like the old saying goes, pray over your home and lock the doors.

This is not about creating or planning for the fall, but it is being grounded and protected in the physical world where things happen, things go awry, and people back out on their words. The beauty of this is you may never have to use the protection. When you know you are fully ready to safeguard yourself, your life, your livelihood and your family, you live your life with more freedom and joy because you are not worrying about the bad things that could happen. The smart CEO prepares for the worst-case scenario and has a plan. Imagine traveling cross country. You would never jump on the road without a map, a full tank of gas and a packed bag. When you know you have everything covered and have that plan and protection, you can relax and enjoy the ride.

It is amazing how many people are surprised when bad things happen. Emergencies, accidents, contract problems, etc are oftentimes avoidable. If it is not avoidable, then the damage can be lessened by your readiness. I may not be able to avoid a massive brush fire from destroying my home but I can make sure that I have my yard well landscaped so there are no dead brush or overgrown vegetation that may add fuel to the fire. I can place important documents and keepsakes in a fire proof safe and assure that I have the proper insurance. If you are ready, then you take care of situations as they come and it does not need to disrupt your life. It is true you can't plan for everything but the more you are prepared and smart, the less you will be thrown off you're A game in life.

Twenty

BOUNDARIES

"Compassionate people ask for what they need. They say no when they need to, and when they say yes, they mean it. They're compassionate because their boundaries keep them out of resentment."

~ Brené Brown ~

BOUNDARIES

"If you are ruthless in your actions, you don't need to be ruthless with your words." This powerful quote holds a significant meaning when it comes to setting boundaries. Boundaries, set by the CEO, are not only important for maintaining healthy relationships but also for taking control of our lives. However, communicating these boundaries can be tricky, but it's essential to be clear and direct without being hurtful or rude.

Setting boundaries is all about protecting your physical, emotional, and mental well-being. It's about putting limits that prevent others from crossing your personal space. Without boundaries, you may feel overwhelmed, taken advantage of, and even resentful towards others. By taking control of your boundaries, you prioritize your own needs and make sure you are not constantly sacrificing your own happiness for the sake of others.

Communicating boundaries effectively is crucial. The key is to be clear and concise. Speak up and express your needs without making excuses or apologizing. For instance, you can say something like, "I'm not comfortable discussing my personal life with coworkers," or "I need some time alone to recharge after a long day."

It's important to note that setting boundaries doesn't mean you're controlling others. It's about taking responsibility for your own well-being. When you prioritize your needs, you create a healthy distance that allows you to maintain your happiness, sanity, and emotional stability.

Saying no and setting boundaries can be challenging, especially if you're used to pleasing everyone. It can be tough to say no to someone you care about or respect. However, being honest and direct with your boundaries is a sign of respect for yourself and others. It's always better to say no upfront than to agree to something you're uncomfortable with and end up breaking your word later.

Setting boundaries is vital for self-care and maintaining healthy relationships. By being direct and respectful with your boundaries, you create a safe and supportive environment for yourself and those around you. Remember, "If you are ruthless in your actions, you don't need to be ruthless with your words." Be willing to walk away, remove access or enforce any other appropriate boundaries. Stay true to your needs and values, and the right people will respect and support your boundaries.

I LOVE ME MORE

As I watched Sex and the City, I couldn't help but be moved by Samantha's powerful words. As she broke up with her handsome but unsuitable boyfriend, he asks “You don't love me anymore?” She responds to him saying “I'm going to say the thing we’re not supposed to say . . . I love Me more”. It was a line that resonated with me deeply. Love starts from within, and if we don't love ourselves first, we can never truly love anyone else.

When we put ourselves first, we fill up with love and a sense of fulfillment that radiates from us. It's from this overflowing place that we can give freely and abundantly. We're not depleted by our giving because we're giving from a place of abundance.

However, when we neglect ourselves and continue to give to others, we risk depleting our own resources. We can only run on fumes for so long before we eventually crash and burn.

As a CEO, it's imperative to take care of your own needs first and assert them when necessary. This not only benefits you, but it also creates space for the nurturing and loving aspects of yourself to thrive.

The Mother and High Priestess archetypes within us thrive when we take care of ourselves. They are the parts of us that want to love and be loved, to give and receive, to nurture and be nurtured. By prioritizing our own needs, we create space for these aspects of ourselves to flourish.

So, take a page from Samantha's book and love yourself more. It's not selfish or wrong to put yourself first. In fact, it's necessary for your own well-being and for the well-being of those around you. When you love yourself, you create an overflow of love and abundance that can be shared with the world.

SETTING BOUNDARIES WITH KIDS

I had a client, we’ll call her Maria, who said that anytime she said No to her kids, they would come back at her, asking again continually, nagging, begging, kicking and screaming just to get her attention until she had just had it and wanted to explode. She wanted to stand in her truth yet couldn't, because they would push her to the edge. Kids have to be trained, especially when you haven't set any boundaries, and especially when you have taught them to ignore what you say. The first step is to make a decision, you must have conviction because as any parent will understand, you will be going into battle. You can ease into this by choosing something manageable to set a clear boundary around and slowly build up your muscles.

When you make a request, make sure they follow through and be persistent where they will abide by your rules or suffer the consequences. And be prepared to enforce the consequences. When my son was young, he picked up a toy at Target and played with it the entire shopping trip. When it came to the checkout lanes, he asked to purchase it. I said not today. He wasn't happy with my answer and began to plead. I repeated "not today" and his pleads became louder until he adamantly yelled, "I want this now". At two years old, he slowly built up his yelling until he was screaming. I took the toy from his hand and nervously ran through the checkout lanes, hurriedly paid and ran out of the store quickly to avoid having everyone in the store staring at me while he was throwing his tantrum. I was mortified but proud of myself for not giving in to his tantrum.

I realized I had to do something different, so the next trip to the store, I prepared him by letting him know my expectations. I told him that if he found something he liked, he can look, but when we left the area, he had to leave the toy. If he didn't listen or raised his voice, kicked, screamed or anything else, we would leave the store immediately. I knew he would test me, so I was ready. I planned a trial run. We took a trip to Target at a time when I was prepared to leave. I didn't really need anything so I wouldn't be inconvenienced if we had to leave. This trip was strictly for practice setting boundaries.

We went through the toy aisle and as expected, he found a toy he had to have. I acknowledged it was a great toy and that we were not going to buy it today. He proceeded to kick and scream. I asked him nicely once to stop or we will leave the store. He ignored me and yelled “I want my toy”. I picked him up, and we quickly left the store and went home. We never had a problem after that.

If you need your children to do something, like clean their room or make their bed, offer a simple command. An example would be "Brandon, I need you to make your bed now." These are the words of a CEO in action, and she means business. She knows that if she doesn't enforce her requests and commands, her son will not take her seriously. Too many times, she has asked him to make his bed and walked away, only to find it still unmade. But not anymore.

As a mother, she believes in giving her son choices and requests when she is ready to accept a yes or no answer. However, when it comes to certain tasks, like making his bed, there is no room for negotiation. She understands that children need to learn that their parents are not kidding, and follow-through is key.

So, when she tells her son to make his bed, she stands there until he does it, even if it means holding his hand and guiding him through the process. For her, it's a matter of asserting her needs and making sure they are met. She knows the importance of choosing her battles wisely. When it comes to tasks that require her physical presence, like picking up dirty clothes or making the bed, she is willing to do it herself or guide her child through the process. This way, there is no room for compromise or negotiation.

It's essential to provide requests and commands when they are necessary, without giving children the option of saying no. For example, instead of asking, "Will you please take out the trash?" she suggests saying, "Would you like to take out the trash now or after dinner?" A command means telling them what to do without compromise. It's the CEO's job to ensure follow-through. It's crucial to stick to your word and not get angry. When you choose to engage in a battle, be ready to follow through. Giving in teaches children that persistence pays off, which undermines the authority of the parent.

Discipline is essential because it provides safety for children. They need structure and boundaries to feel secure. When a mother fails to honor her word, children feel unsafe and unsure of who to trust. Building trust and respect takes time, but it's worth the effort. Don't feel guilty for disciplining your children. As a mother, you have the responsibility to provide structure and discipline, and it's your duty to follow through. Start slowly, choose your battles wisely, and build from there. Soon, your children will learn to respect you, and you'll feel confident in your role as CEO of your household.

Twenty-one

SPEAK UP DARLING

"When the whole world is silent, even one voice becomes powerful"
~ Malala Yousafzai ~

ASKING FOR WHAT YOU WANT

I was chaperoning a school dance one evening and received a text from a male friend of mine. It was a typical "what are you doing?" text. This was from a man whom I had been seeing sporadically, however, we were not in a relationship yet. As a woman in my feminine energy, I was patiently waiting while throwing out some hints that if he wanted something more, I would definitely be open. I responded that I was at a school dance and asked him what he was doing. He was watching a basketball game, a pastime he loved. I said, "you know, you should come and join us". It definitely wasn't a request. It was the sassy Playmate and the confident CEO that was asking him to come with me. It was a little flirtatious and my first attempt at getting him to take initiative to see me.

We texted back and forth for a while yet he never gave me an answer. At one point he said, call me when you're done and we'll meet up for a drink. For a moment I thought, hell no. I don't want to make myself that easy. If he is courting me, he should court me, not arrange for a late night rendezvous. Even though I was getting frustrated and feeling rejected, I was trying to stay positive and in my feminine, so I asked "does that mean you're not coming?" Again, he wasn't giving me an answer.

I finally realized that I was asking him to come chaperone a high school dance with me. If I were to ask him if he wanted to come and join me, of course he would say no, even I didn't want to be there. So rather than asking him to chaperone the dance with me, I made a much different request. I said "Will you please join me and hang out with me? It would make me very happy." Right away he responded and said, if it makes you happy, I'll be there. And he showed up.

The CEO is smart, she understands the male mind and doesn't take things personally. The girl in me was saying, if you loved me, you would want to spend time with me. But the male mind is very clear, I don't want to go to a school dance. That doesn't sound fun at all. It kind of actually sounds really boring. I had to step into his mind and remember to make him a winner. The way I made him a winner is I used the words "Will you . . . ?" I also told him how he would win by letting him know "It would make me very happy". That was the motivation that allowed him to step up. Now he is my hero because I told him exactly how he can win and make me happy.

He was very sweet throughout the night. He kept asking, "Are you happy? My response was "Can't you tell?" I was a giddy little girl. I kept letting him know that yes, I'm very happy that you came. I thanked him several times. I gave him a big hug and a kiss on the cheek. I kept making him feel like he was my hero that night.

There are certain ways we call out the heroic qualities of the men in our lives. These men can be in our friendships, co-workers, spouse, male children, other family members and even people we meet at the store, restaurant or other places you visit as you go about your day. Instead of taking on the role of the mother and resorting to begging, pleading, coercing, or demanding that your partner do chores or take you out, you want to invite them to step up and be your hero. Making them feel like a hero is about calling out that masculine part of them that wants to protect us, take care of us and make us happy all the while rewarding them well for their gallant acts, however big or small.

COURAGE TO SPEAK

Having the courage to speak up and be heard is paramount to the CEO. Don't censor yourself. Censoring fosters powerlessness. Asking for what you want and standing up for your convictions will benefit not only you but your family, friends, community and the world. The world needs people who have something to say and are not afraid to say it. Saying what you think, even at the risk of disagreeing with others, gives you strength. Trusting your voice allows you to retain your integrity. When you question your words, backpedal or skirt around an issue, you weaken yourself. When you say what you mean and mean what you say, you remain powerful. The courage to speak up provides a woman with authenticity. She can show up, unapologetic, in her full power and be seen for who she truly is, what she thinks and how she feels.

BE IMPECCABLE WITH YOUR WORDS

Don Miguel Ruiz, author of "The Four Agreements" beautifully illustrates the power of language and being impeccable with your words. The CEO is likewise, impeccable with her words. Language is a significant dimension of the CEO because she understands that creation begins with the word. Nothing comes to fruition, nothing gets created, and nothing gets manifested until we put words to it. When she announces a goal to the world, "I will start a successful business in 12 months", every cell of her body aligns to make sure it transpires within that time frame. When she describes something, that description determines her perception of that thing, and ultimately becomes her experience. The CEO understands that a woman doesn't see something and then describes it, in actuality, she describes it first, then is able to see it. Then, it becomes her reality.

The CEO is also mindful of the impact her words have on others. This means no gossiping. Gossip depletes your energy, and causes you to lose trust in yourself. She avoids gossiping and spreading negativity, recognizing that words have the power to build up or tear down. By consciously choosing to use words that uplift and empower, she creates a positive environment in which everyone around her can thrive. This not only benefits others, but it also contributes to the CEO's personal sense of integrity and authenticity.

Twenty-two

YOUR DOMAIN

"Behind every successful woman is a fierce determination to turn her dreams into reality, one goal at a time."

CLEARING CLUTTER

I promise you, if you get organized, clear your clutter and create systems and procedures to streamline your life, you will literally double your results and double your time off. You will be able to accomplish more in less time and have more successes. This takes some work initially, but the benefits far, far outweigh the initial work and time you put in to set everything up.

Take some time to organize your computer. Some of us have computers that look like something just vomited all over it. How often are you spending a minute, 3 minutes, or even 5 minutes looking for a file. That time adds up and takes precious time away from what you would love to go.

I have cleaned out junk drawers and when complete, felt like I could breathe. I was able to relax. It brings a smile to my face and allows more creativity in my life. Just do it and notice how you feel afterward. Clutter is a huge energy drain. Take some time to organize your home and office. Organize your car and your paperwork. Make sure you know where things are in your home, make sure you know where things are in your business. Make sure your important documents get and stay organized. I recently spoke with a client about starting a new business and she mentioned that she spent 45 minutes looking for her son's immunizations record and still couldn't find it. That is valuable time and energy she could have been using to work on building her business. Her assignment . . . get organized. She started in the garage and went through the entire house and now she is well on her way to successfully running her new business. And the icing . . . she was informed that she would get monthly mid four digit checks for a deal she made years ago. Creating room in her life created room for abundance to appear.

The CEO is extremely organized. The CEO knows exactly where things are. This morning my son asked me where the pair of scissors were. I could tell him without skipping a beat. Upstairs, left side of the closet in white dresser, third drawer down. And those scissors go exactly right back to where they were. The CEO has a system. She has a system in place and everything functions in the most efficient way. Stepping into your inner CEO requires you to be extremely organized. This reduces stress and creates more space and time. And lest you think this is too disciplined, so much work and constraining, the Playmate loves it because she has more time to play. The Mother loves it because she can give more without exhaustion and the High Priestess loves it because it allows her more freedom and flow.

INCOMPLETES AND MESSES

The CEO understands the importance of a clean slate. She diligently clears any areas of her life that drain her energy, setting clear boundaries to allow her to focus on her tasks and projects. This is essential if we are to achieve our dreams and move forward towards success. With a clean slate, we can concentrate on what's important, becoming hyper-focused like the masculine energy that zeroes in on a goal or task like a hunter on their prey. This ability to focus is critical when creating our day, our dreams, and achieving our goals. The CEO knows how to remove distractions, messes, and incompletes that drain our power and creativity, leaving us with minor irritations that steal our focus. Things like a cluttered garage, incomplete relationships, or unfinished repairs can sap our life force energy and dilute our ability to create. Over time, these distractions erode our self-confidence, leaving us feeling resigned and distrustful of our abilities. Self trust is lost.

Imagine you're an entrepreneur with ambitious goals, such as earning one million dollars this year or bringing in 20 new clients. You're motivated, focused, and determined to make big things happen. But then, you spend five minutes searching for a pencil or your keys, and your confidence starts to wane. If you can't even keep track of a pencil, how can you expect to achieve your lofty goals?

The truth is, the small, seemingly insignificant things we tolerate or leave unfinished in our lives can have a huge impact on our overall energy and ability to succeed. When you come home to a messy garage or can't find a document you need for a report, you start to feel resigned and defeated. These incompletes and messes drain your energy and leave you feeling hopeless.

Every time you walk by a broken cabinet or think of your incomplete taxes from last year, you lose a bit of your vitality and life force. These small irritations and incomplete tasks slowly but surely sap your energy, leaving you with little left to pursue your dreams. You may find yourself functioning on the leftovers, attempting to live a full and successful life with the crumbs of energy left over.

However, when you start to tackle these incompletes and messes, you begin to replenish your energy and creative power. By clearing your physical and mental space of these draining elements, you allow more ideas, resources, and opportunities to flow into your life. Completing these small tasks not only frees up your energy but also allows you to focus on what is truly important in your life.

The small things we tolerate or leave unfinished in our lives can have a profound impact on our energy and ability to succeed. By clearing our space and completing these tasks, we can reclaim our precious energy and make big things happen in the world. Living from this present state of being allows for more ideas and resources to enter, more innovation and more success.

Be fully present in the moment and take the time to address any unfinished business from the past. Begin by identifying the things that irritate you or need fixing. Are there areas where you could use some help? Perhaps you have unresolved business matters, like outstanding debts or invoices. Maybe your closet is overflowing with clothes or your garage is disorganized. Do you have tax records that are in disarray, or junk drawers filled with items you can never find when you need them? Are there missing or broken items that need fixing, or maintenance issues that need addressing?

It's important to acknowledge the weight that these unfinished tasks can have on us and our ability to move forward. By taking the time to make a list of everything that needs to be fixed, cleared, or organized, you can begin to lighten your load. Even though it may seem overwhelming, simply getting everything out of your head and onto paper is a step forward. This will allow you to focus your energy on the present and move towards achieving your goals without the distractions of unfinished tasks weighing you down. So take some time this week to walk through your home or business and make that list. Remember, it's the first step towards lightening your load and freeing up your energy for the things that matter most. You no longer have to hold it in your mind or your heart.

I had a water leak in the wall in my upstairs bathroom which eventually leaked through the top of the stairs. It created a brown water stain in my staircase. I didn't think much about getting it fixed or painted over. It was just a little water stain after all, no big deal. But I noticed that every time I walked up the stairs, my attention went directly to the stain. That was constantly draining my energy because I walk up and down those stairs several times throughout the day. Each time, there is a part of me that says eww, even for just that split second, my energy drops. That is something that went on my list soon thereafter.

Take an hour of your time to go through your house and make your list. Is there a little part of your wall that needs to be painted because somebody scratched it? Is there a broken lamp? Is there a stain somewhere? Is there something that isn't working or that needs to be fixed? Does the garage need to be organized or is the hallway closet filled with junk? Write down your list and make a point to start to check off items on that list. Notice how much free time you create for yourself once you check off all those items. After cleaning up my linen closet, I noticed the smile that comes across my face every time I open the doors. I feel my energy uplifted. It is a tangible feeling and will open up so much more beautiful life energy throughout your day. Notice how light and clear you feel, not only when you complete it but every time you look at something that is now beautiful, clean and organized. I was so much happier cooking when all my pots, pans and kitchen items were beautifully arranged. Not only did it make me feel great while I was in the kitchen, but it saved me so much time and made it easier to whip up something fabulous.

In order to take a little pressure off and be more efficient, group like items together. Group items that a handyman can complete all in one day. You can hire someone for the day or lovingly hand off your honey do list to your man if he loves fixing things. If he doesn't, don't feel any guilt over hiring someone. The abundance that will follow this drain will more than pay for hiring someone for the day. If he loves fixing things, bring out your inner Playmate and lovingly ask him. Allow him to be your hero and reward him accordingly.

SETTING GOALS

The CEO is a master at setting and achieving goals. Setting goals is an essential aspect of achieving success in both personal and professional life. Without clear goals, we may find ourselves wandering aimlessly without a sense of direction or purpose. It is important to have a clear vision for what we want to achieve, and create a plan to get there.

So, how can we set and achieve our own goals? This is an area we can dive more deeply into and I take my clients through a specific step by step process but there are some general guidelines. The first step is to clearly define what it is that you want to achieve. This means identifying specific outcomes that you want to accomplish. For example, if you want to start your own business, your goal might be to generate $100,000 in revenue within the first year. Once you have defined your goals, the next step is to make them as specific as possible. This means defining exactly what it is that you want to achieve, and how you will measure your progress towards that goal. For example, your goal might be to generate $100,000 in revenue within the first year by acquiring 100 new customers. Once you have defined your specific goals, it's time to create a plan to achieve them. This means breaking down your goal into smaller, more manageable tasks, and creating a timeline for completing each task. For example, your plan might include developing a marketing strategy, building a website, and reaching out to potential customers each with its own deadline.

With your plan in place, it's time to take action. This means putting in the work required to achieve your goals. It's important to stay motivated and focused, and to track your progress along the way. And finally, as you work towards your goals, review your progress regularly and adjust your plan as needed. This means reflecting on what is working and what is not, and making changes to your approach as needed. With dedication and persistence, the CEO can achieve anything she sets her mind to.

Twenty-three

MONEY AND POWER

"Financial empowerment is about having the courage to overcome your fears and take control of your life. It's about having the freedom to make choices and create a future that aligns with your values and dreams."

~ Suze Orman ~

DATE YOUR DOLLARS

Prosperity, abundance and money all come from the strong CEO. The CEO is responsible for everything financial, making money, keeping track of her assets, and creating financial freedom. She is aware of her income, net worth, how to increase her earnings, where her finances are allocated, and maintains complete control over her wealth portfolio.

I once heard a woman say she dates her dollars and I loved that idea. I have adopted a "date my dollars" ritual and I prescribe it to all my clients. I set up a ritual around paying my bills, balancing my checkbook, looking at my income and expenses as well as investments. This allows me to stay on top of my finances so I always know where I stand.

Once a week I date my dollars. Just like developing a relationship with something that is important, I create a beautiful ritual so that it raises the vibration of my money. Oftentimes when we think of money or paying bills, we get stressed, we get discouraged and we contract. We have a repulsive feeling around money and I assure you, money feels it. When we create positive feelings around money, love becoming a master manager of our money and become empowered around money, money begins to naturally flow to you. You become a powerful magnet for money.

I would suggest you choose a special time when you won't be interrupted, have a glass of wine or a cup of tea. I usually do it on the weekend in the morning. I have my tea and a little biscotti. I bring out my laptop, my bills, my mail from the week, and I go through everything. I set up the majority of my bills to be taken from my account automatically to save time and streamline my life. I balance my checking account, pay my bills, catalogue what I earned and what I spent. Look at my investments, how they are doing and I set any financial intentions. If I notice my credit card debt is high, I set an intention to pay them off by a certain date and set up a plan. I use Quicken to keep track of my finances but there are many free options and spreadsheets you can use.

Every time I pay my bill, I write a thank you in the notes column of the ledger. When I pay my electric bill, even though it comes out of my account automatically, I write "Thank you for my electricity" in the notes column. When I pay my mortgage, I write "Thank you for my home", etc. When I have income, I write "Thank you for the money or thank you for the opportunity to serve".

I am very clear on what I have, what is going out, and what is coming in. I will tell you, it was very scary initially, so I get your hesitation. It was so much easier to live in denial, to not look and pray that my credit card works every time I swipe it. I have been there many times before I got a handle on my money.

I said it was easier, but I understand it is not comfortable. In fact, the stress of living this way can eat away at you and your finances. Even when I was in the red, it was better to know where I stood than to live in denial, knowing in my heart I was digging myself deeper into a hole. It's easy to avoid looking at our money, especially when we don't have much, but that's the worst thing we can do. Knowing where our money is going allows us to take control of our finances. I'm not a big believer in budget, because to me, budgeting is very constraining. Awareness, however, allows me more freedom. When I know exactly where my money is going, I start to make different decisions. If I see that I've spent a lot of money at Starbucks this month, the equivalent of a couple of new outfits, I may think twice the next time I have to choose between making coffee at home or stopping at a Starbucks.

Many women tend to hand off the finances to their husbands or to the men in their life. If you want to create prosperity, you must know everything there is to know about where you stand and have access to it, even if someone else is taking care of it. If you're running a business, you need to be on top of your money because there is a tendency to look at cashflow without balancing the influx and the outflow of money. You never really know where you stand and you think you're doing well. You may have a huge expenditure, but without knowing where the leaks are, you may find yourself one invoice away from going out of business. Even if you have a financial planner, a CFO or an accountant, it is imperative that you regularly sit down with them, know where your money is and never give up control.

Many people misunderstand and misquote bible verses when it comes to money. They often quote "Money is the root of all evil." However, the actual bible verse is "For the love of money is a root of all kinds of evils." Money itself is neutral; it is simply a tool and a resource. The real problem arises when we become obsessed with money and it starts to control us. When we play the "money may I" game, we let our bank account determine what we can or can't have. We might say things like, "I don't have enough money to take that vacation" or "I can't afford to buy that new coat." In this scenario, money is in control of us, dictating our decisions and limiting our possibilities. Money becomes our master. Some people may even be indebted to a Master-card.

Instead, the CEO should strive to be the master of money and use it as a tool to achieve our goals and dreams. By taking control of our finances and viewing money as a neutral resource, we can avoid pushing it away and instead use it to create a fulfilling life.

So part of mastering money is being aware of it, being in control of it, making powerful decisions with it and directing money to support us. No longer playing the "money may I game". Instead, we make a decision such as "I want to travel to Italy next year", and as the master, I decide to put away 5% of my check every month. Or as the master, I decide and take action on putting away 20% of my income every money for my investment portfolio. Making powerful decisions with our money is a critical aspect of mastering it. This means investing wisely, saving for the future, and making informed decisions about our financial future. It's about taking calculated risks and making investments that will provide long-term benefits. As we become more responsible and in charge, more money will flow to our hands.

Directing our money to support us is the ultimate goal. This means using our money to create the life we want, whether that's through investing in our education, starting a business, or pursuing our passions. It's about using our financial resources to build the life we've always dreamed of. Mastering money is not an easy task, but with awareness, control, powerful decision-making, and intentional direction, it is possible to achieve financial success and live the life we want.

DITCH THE BITCH

Too often, women feel the need to prove themselves at work. If they are accomplished and determined, they feel they must compete with men who work around them. The men seem to have a natural ability to compete, be single focused, get the job done while maintaining an aura of calm abandon. Women, on the other hand, especially those that are hard working and determined, forcefully attempt to hide their feminine traits and become the "man" at the workplace. We show up early, stay late, multi-task, take on more than we can handle and say yes to all requests. All while maintaining a very serious demeanor.

One of my first jobs was working at a non-profit agency. I was truly excited about taking on this job because I spent a number of years throughout high school and college volunteering for this agency and was thrilled to be able to earn a living doing what I love to do full time. On my first day, I walked into the reception area, a huge smile on my face and a lightness to my step and was greeted by the CEO whom I had met briefly during my volunteer days. He gave me a warm welcome while hiding a worried look on his face. He was flanked by two men I had never met. The receptionist quickly told me where to meet my supervisor and I excused myself and left.

My second day on the job, I was told that the CEO was removed from his position by the board. I didn't understand what was going on but didn't ask many questions. I began my exciting job of setting up programs and services, recruiting youth volunteers, planning leadership development trainings and networking with various agencies and community members. Three months went by and our agency ran like clockwork. Everyone was truly dedicated to their job and was committed to serving the community. It was a joyful place to work. On any evening, you would observe staff staying late on their own time working to go above and beyond what their job description entailed. It was a truly inspiring place to work and the difference we made in the community reflected that level of dedication and commitment. Our in house maintenance man was an undercover chef and provided special treats for the staff at least once a week. We acknowledged each other's birthdays, special family celebrations and Friday happy hours.

Three months later, the board announced they found a replacement for the CEO who would begin shortly. It was a woman from another office who had a great deal of experience in this type of organization. We were all excited to welcome a new leader who would share the commitment, dedication and positive dynamics of the current department. A staff meeting was scheduled on her first day. We met in the boardroom: everyone seated around a large table, a buzz of excitement filled the air as everyone was happy to see her.

She walked in silently and sat down at the head of the table. Hello, my name is Cruella DeVille (not her real name for obvious reasons). The very next words that followed were "If you stab me in the back, I'll stab you in the gut". The silence in the room was deafening, and no one even dared to exchange glances. We were all shocked. This sentiment truly came out of nowhere. All I thought was now that's a woman who is threatened. She was obviously successful in her line of work but failed to develop any social or leadership skills. She was demanding, condescending, focused on the negative and never acknowledging the good work anyone did.

When women fought for equality, we were finally given the space, freedom and acknowledgement that we so well deserved. Feminine energy elevates any organization with its ability to build relationships, solve problems, and offer unique perspectives and emotional intelligence. Yet, unfortunately, some women decided to abandon these traits and become their version of a "man".

However, this comes at a cost. Women who abandon their feminine qualities to "fit in" to a man's world lose their unique strengths and perspectives. This not only limits their own potential but also limits the potential of the organization they work for. It can have negative effects on her well-being and sense of self. She may feel like she has to suppress a part of herself to be accepted or respected in the workplace, leading to feelings of disconnection and internal conflict. This can also lead to burnout, as she may feel like she is constantly working against her natural tendencies and trying to fit into a mold that is not authentic to her. When a woman is not able to fully express and utilize her feminine qualities, she may not be able to contribute to the workplace in the way she is truly capable of, leading to feelings of frustration and unfulfillment. When women embrace their authentic selves and bring their full range of qualities and strengths to the workplace, they create a more dynamic and powerful environment for all. So ditch the bitch and embrace your fabulousness.

CEO CONCLUSION

The CEO is about doing. She is connected to the earth, and requires grounding for everything to flourish. She moves mountains and turns possibilities into probabilities. If you want to bring in more of the CEO, get something done on a material level. This is the physical aspect of a woman, the masculine energy, so being out in the earth touching the grass or being in nature with trees will help you reconnect with your CEO.

When you need to rebalance the CEO or bring in more of her energy, set some boundaries, say "no" more often, clean out a drawer, clean out your wallet, or get a project that you've been procrastinating on done. Start to honor yourself and your needs, deliberately and carefully choose your words so that everything that comes out of your mouth is 100% true and something you are willing to back up and follow through.

Ways to get in touch with the CEO

- Set a specific goal and develop an action plan to achieve it
- Seek feedback and constructive criticism from a trusted colleague
- Take a calculated risk
- Try one new thing
- Practice saying no in the mirror
- Develop a morning routine to set the tone for your day
- Delegate one new task
- Clean out a drawer
- Clean out your wallet
- Go out into nature

PART V

Twenty-four

THE HIGH PRIESTESS

"When a woman steps into her inner High Priestess, she embraces her innate power, allure, grace, and wisdom. She becomes the queen of her own life, ruling with compassion, courage, and confidence. She moves through the world with a regal elegance, commanding respect and radiating beauty. She knows her worth, she trusts her intuition, and she leads with love. She is a force to be reckoned with, and she is unstoppable in her pursuit of greatness."

THE HIGH PRIESTESS

The final Feminine type that makes a woman a Queen is the High Priestess. This is the aspect of the woman that is deeply connected with the power within her. She is centered and knows who she is on a very deep, powerful level. She can walk in the room and all eyes turn to her without ever having to say a word. She has a deep spiritual connection. She knows she has access to a great strength within her that is more powerful than her personal day to day experience. She may call it Source, God, Allah, Yahweh, the Universe or the God of her heart. Her inner strength comes from that place of knowing who she is and where she comes from. Embodying the High Priestess is what makes a woman alluring and mysterious because there is a part of her that is untouchable and unaffected.

Like a Queen, she doesn't need to fight for anything and her every wish or desire becomes a command. This power and strength within becomes the foundation for her actions and interactions, how she relates with other people, her behaviors and her identity. She has conviction over her beliefs and is willing to stand by them. She is loyal, protective and self-assured. While the CEO runs the show, the High Priestess creates space for the show. She is a visionary, the aspect of the woman that holds intention and a higher vision. The High Priestess exudes grace and a calm self-assurance of someone who is certain of her own self-worth. She is able to present herself and choose words to express her points of view in a powerful, elegant and graceful manner. She never engages in gossip, negative interactions or confrontations, is loyal and mild mannered. She stands tall, graceful and elegant. She treats everyone with the utmost respect and always remembers her manners. She never raises her voice and is a lady in every sense of the word.

OUT OF SYNC

I love the High Priestess, and I know many women who are drawn to my work have a great resonance for the High Priestess. Before we get deeper into who she is, what she embodies and how she shows up in the world, let's talk about how we know when the High Priestess is out of sync.

The High Priestess is the Feminine Type that allows us to be deeply connected to the power within ourselves. She is the part of us that has access to source, strength from within. That being said, we know when the High Priestess within us is out of sync if we are feeling unfulfilled. If you ever feel like you are just going through the motions in your relationships, your career, and your day, and there is a sense of feeling unfulfilled, the High Priestess within is out of harmony. There is not a clear connection to the "Why" of the actions you are taking. You may feel as if there is nothing at the end of the tunnel for you. You may feel as if you are stuck in a rat race, going through the motions with no real connection to a purpose. You may have even asked yourself, "What is this all for?" "Am I getting something from this?" If you are feeling unfulfilled, then the High Priestess within you is definitely out of sync.

The second way to determine if the High Priestess is not reigning in your life is being and or feeling ungrounded. You feel like you are at the whims of all the energy around you. You wake up, you go through your day, and how you feel is dependent on the mood of other people, dependent on the weather, dependent on the current state of the economy or government, your boss or your clients. You get thrown around quite a bit. You are not in a centered state. For example, today was a good day because no one upset you or today was a good day because there were not a lot of expectations placed upon you. Conversely, you may feel today was not a good day because your customer or your boss was upset. You may have had a rough day because your kids got in trouble at school or because your husband didn't call when he knew he was going to be late for dinner. This is a clear indication that you are at the effect of the people and circumstances outside of you rather than rooted in your own strength. You may feel that life happens to you, with drama after drama throwing you off your grounding. If you feel ungrounded and you are at the effect of the outside situations in the world, then your High Priestess is out of sync.

The same is true when you are being reactive. Things happen and you are reacting, and chasing or running away from them. I was at a hockey game recently watching the Anaheim Ducks play against the Edmonton Oilers. It had been about 20 years since I had gone to a game. I used to attend them all the time when my son was younger and loved the game. I was not a big fan then and didn't always enjoy the game. It was hard for me to follow the puck and because we had seats so close to the rink, the puck was lost on me quite often.

This time however, we had seats higher up in the stadium so I had a better vantage point of the entire ice rink and enjoyed it much more. I was able to follow the puck and the players. What I noticed right off the bat during the first quarter was that the Ducks were chasing the puck. Wherever the puck went, they chased after it. When the puck went over to the left side of the rink, they went to the left, when it went to the right, they swerved to the right. They were always just a bit shy of catching up to it. The Oilers, on the other hand, had a different strategy. I noticed they went to where the puck was going. I was happy to share my brilliant observation with my son. I also shared the great Wayne Gretzky quote. I said, you know, Wayne Gretzky was great because he always played where the puck was going to be, not where it was. My son kind of laughed at me and shared that Gretzky played with the Oilers. So obviously, there is something about this team. They know and are well trained on how to play where the puck is going.

The same idea applies in our life. To re-act means acting again. You are participating in the same actions over and over again, the actions that have been programmed into you. Now you simply play the recording without much thought. So, are you reacting, chasing or running away from situations that get thrown at you, or are you creating your life? Are you setting an intention or do you fall victim to life with all its twists and turns? Are you getting pushed into the same emotions over and over again? If something is out of balance with you, do you take a moment to center before you act or are you reactive?

The High Priestess has the ability to slow time down. When you're out of sync with the High Priestess, you might find yourself feeling frazzled, rushed, or overwhelmed. You might notice that your thoughts are scattered and that you're having trouble focusing on what really matters. However, when you tap into the energy of the High Priestess, you'll find that time seems to slow down, allowing you to be more present and focused. You'll feel more in tune with your intuition and inner wisdom, and you'll be better able to navigate life's challenges with ease and grace. Whether you're facing a big decision or just trying to get through your to-do list, the High Priestess can help you stay centered, calm, and confident.

Are you searching outside of yourself for answers, looking outside of you to direct you, to determine where you should go and what you should do? Are you searching outside of yourself for a sense of fulfillment, a sense of purpose, for something or someone to make you happy? The High Priestess does not look outside of her for anything. She always looks within. She looks within for answers. She looks within for information. She looks within for insight as to which direction to go. The CEO within her may seek guidance and information from trusted sources, however, the High Priestess checks in to connect with her truth as she sifts through all the resources.

If you are feeling sad or empty for prolonged periods of time, then the High Priestess is out of sync. This is not to say that sadness is an undesired emotion. We naturally feel sad when we have lost something or someone. It is okay to feel this. However, if the emotion lingers far after the event or circumstance has passed or seems to be your prevailing emotion, then this is cause for attention. The sadness and emptiness may be a sign of disconnection to the source of love, power and all that is. When I looked at the energy of my clients who were suffering from depression, the primary thing that popped out was that they were not connected to their source. That disconnection was creating a sense of separation and hence causing a feeling of depression. These emotions; sadness, depression, low energy, and emptiness is what prevails when the High Priestess is not in alignment.

DO YOU KNOW WHO I AM

The High Priestess is deeply connected with the power that is within her. (You will hear this quite often in this chapter). She knows who she is on a very deep, powerful level. If you think of an actual Queen in a Monarch, it is her birthright to be a Queen. It is her birthright to rule. She is a Queen simply because she exists. She may have been given that role at birth or she may have married a King and hence became a Queen. She can walk through her lands and all bow to her because of who she is, who she is connected to. She does not have to assert her power. She does not have to fight for power. She does not have to earn respect or veneration. She is connected to something powerful, which is the King, her father or her husband. So simply by virtue of her birth or marriage, she holds this title and steps into it with grace and reverence.

The High Priestess within us, the Queen within us, knows that just by virtue of our birth, just by virtue of who we are, we are connected to something deep and powerful and we show up that way. We live our life that way. There is nothing to prove. There is nothing to fight for. There is nothing to struggle with.

She has a radiance about her because there is a source of light and strength which comes from within. When deeply connected, she can walk in a room and light up the room without ever having to say a word. All eyes turn to her, captivated by her radiance. Her light and presence is palpable because of her deep, spiritual connection. She knows she has access to a great strength within her that is more powerful than anything outside of her. This is her quiet strength. She is not shoving or pushing her weight around. She is not fighting for attention, speaking loudly over others and doesn't have to try to take up space. She has a deep, inner knowing.

Because she has that inner knowing, because she has that strength, because she has a power and strength from deep within, then that becomes the foundation for all of her actions and her interactions. It becomes a foundation for how she relates to other people. It becomes the foundation for all her behaviors and her identity.

SPIRITUAL PRACTICE

In order for the High Priestess to develop and maintain her power and connection, she requires a daily spiritual practice. The spiritual practice may look different depending on who you are, your belief systems and your preferences. Just as you would shower every day to maintain that fresh, clean feeling, a daily spiritual practice is something a woman should never skip or skimp on. These include small, everyday rituals that clear the noise and clutter of the chaotic world, connect you to a deeper purpose, and help bring peace and comfort to your life. These daily rituals nurture your deep inner being and connect you to your deeper self.

I offer powerful meditations in this book and others you can access for free and in my programs. Meditation is a spiritual practice that knows no religious or cultural boundaries. Meditation is the act of listening, raising your awareness and connecting to the deepest part of you. When you meditate, you shut out the external world, where you are at the effect of your environment along with the people in it, and you connect to your internal world, where your true power lies. Disconnecting from the senses that connect you to the external world is crucial to powerfully connect with your internal world. By closing your eyes and finding a quiet space, you allow yourself to tune out external stimuli and focus on your inner self. As one of my meditation teachers used to tell me, closing your eyes is probably the most difficult part of the work we are going to do because this is where you claim for yourself and announce to the world on an energetic level that you are taking this time for yourself, blocking out the noise of the world with all its distractions and demands, and focusing 100% on you.

Because women tend to give so much to everyone around them, in order to honor yourself as a woman, you need to take time to recharge, guilt free. Ironically, this gives you more to give to others, but without depleting your energy. You are the most important person here and you are definitely required to take time for yourself. During your meditation, breathe deeply. We women forget to breathe sometimes. Taking long deep breaths fills your soul on a beautiful level. Gift this time to yourself.

When you complete your time in meditation, you will want to replenish your space. As you go through your day, oftentimes, you leave little bits of you, little bits of your energy in various places. Perhaps you had a conversation that was particularly emotional and you left part of your energy in that interaction. Many people, especially women, leave parts of themselves at work. You may have part of your energy still working out a problem. This causes you to feel scattered and ungrounded. Calling back all of your energy will allow you to feel powerful, whole, and complete.

This tool provides an avenue to release quite a bit of energy that is not yours around being a woman. This release creates a void. Simply by raising your consciousness, increasing your awareness of where you are, you begin to let go of that which no longer serves you. Releasing this energy that you may have been holding on to for quite a while creates a void so it's important to fill that void with your own energy, and bring back your own essence.

CONNECTION TO SOURCE

The High Priestess possesses an innate and unwavering sense of knowing that is deeply rooted in her connection to a higher power. She has powerful intuition. This is unlike a Mother's intuition which is focused on reading the energy and emotions of others through somatic cues. The way the Mother connects is through energy cords, reading the aura, and having telepathic communication.

The High Priestess, on the other hand, taps into a more profound level of intuition that is connected to the universe itself. Her intuition comes from God, the Universe, the Cosmos, Universal Intelligence, Universal Power or whatever you would like to call it. The High Priestess's intuition is not limited to the physical realm, but rather extends beyond it. Her intuition transcends the physical and is attuned to the true essence of things, giving her the ability to see beyond the surface level of situations and circumstances. She has access to a higher level of consciousness and is able to tap into universal knowledge that goes beyond what can be observed or experienced in the physical world.

This means that she can perceive and understand things that others cannot, and she has the ability to see through illusions and to discern what is truly important. Her intuition is not clouded by personal biases or emotions, but rather is grounded in a deep understanding of the nature of reality. By accessing this universal information, she is able to gain insights and knowledge that is not limited by time or space, and her intuition becomes a powerful tool for navigating the complexities of life.

This allows her to make wise decisions, to see things from multiple perspectives, and to navigate complex situations with ease. Because of her connection to the universal source of knowledge and wisdom, the High Priestess is able to guide others towards their highest potential, helping them to find their true purpose and to live a fulfilling and meaningful life.

Twenty-five

GRACEFUL ENTRY

"Choose your intention carefully and then practice holding your consciousness to it, so it becomes the guiding light in your life."

~ Roger Delano Hinkins ~

RISE AND SHINE

As the sun slowly rises over the horizon, most people jump right into their day, checking their phones, responding to emails, and getting ready for work. But for many successful women, the first hour of the day is reserved for something much more important - themselves.

It's a simple concept, really. By taking time each morning to meditate, journal, connect with their needs, desires, wisdom and internal resources, women are able to start their day with clarity, focus and intention. This hour is not just about self-care, but also about setting the stage for a successful, productive day ahead.

Women who prioritize this first hour for themselves understand the importance of creating a sacred space to connect with their inner selves, their inner High Priestess. This could mean waking up early, finding a quiet corner of their home, or even taking a walk in nature to clear their minds and set intentions for the day.

During this hour, meditation is a crucial practice. By focusing on their breath and clearing their minds, women are able to tap into a deep sense of calm and clarity that sets the tone for the day ahead. They may also use this time to visualize their goals and affirmations, setting powerful intentions for the day and beyond.

Journaling is another important tool for women during this sacred hour. By putting pen to paper, they are able to connect with their inner wisdom, express their thoughts and feelings, and explore their desires and dreams. This process of self-reflection is powerful, allowing them to gain insight into their deepest selves and the path forward.

Connecting with their needs and desires is also a crucial component of this first hour. By tuning into their intuition, women are able to understand what they truly need and desire, and make choices that align with their values and goals. This may mean setting boundaries with work, prioritizing self-care, or simply taking time for things that bring them joy.

During this sacred hour, women are able to tap into their internal resources - their strength, resilience, and creativity - that will help them navigate whatever challenges may come their way throughout the day. By connecting with these inner resources, they are able to face the day with confidence and grace.

The practice of saving the first hour for oneself is a powerful tool for Queens who want to create a life of purpose, intention, and fulfillment. By prioritizing their own needs and desires, they are able to show up fully for themselves and for others, making a powerful impact in the world. So tomorrow, when the sun rises, take the time to connect with your inner self and start your day with intention. You'll be amazed at what you can achieve.

PRESENCE

There is a true classiness about the High Priestess. There is an epidemic in today's world where people are constantly getting distracted, multi-tasking and checking multiple social media platforms. In meetings, people often pull out their cell phones and have it on their table checking it throughout the meeting. That is something a High Priestess would never do because the High Priestess is fully present to the meeting, the agenda and the people around her. When somebody pulls out a cell phone, it sends the message that there is something more important than what is present. As she is disconnecting from the group, it sends the message that you are not important. People may feel they are multi-tasking but as we discussed with the CEO, multi-tasking makes you less productive and creates more stress.

I have heard from numerous sources that Bill Clinton has an amazing ability to be fully present with each person he is talking with. When Bill Clinton is talking to you, you feel like you are the only person in that room. It does not matter if there is a whole line of people or even a crowd around you. As he is engaged with you, he makes you feel as if you were the most important person at that time. That is what the High Priestess does to every person she touches. Every experience is elevated with her touch and her attention. She elevates every person around her, and makes them feel valued, cherished and important.

QUIET QUEEN ENERGY

The High Priestess has a stillness, a quiet strength to her. She easily and regularly connects within, to the power source that comes from a deepness inside her heart and soul. To access this strength, a quiet, still practice is required; time away from the noise of the world, the chaos of other people's negativity and the turmoil caused by the breakdown in society's moral compass. A Queen regularly takes time to return to her chamber, her sanctuary, that place she can access her own inner voice and her inner strength.

To help you feel peaceful and centered, begin by spending some time in the quiet stillness. Meditation or silence has been lauded for centuries as the way to listen to and access the power within. If you have a practice, commit to it daily. If you have yet to adopt one, you may simply sit in silence, feeling your body as you breathe in and out. You may recite a mantra and then go into silence or you may follow a number of meditation practices, one of which I have laid out in this chapter.

PACE OF POWER

For the successful CEO, she can easily be caught up in a world where everyone is in a rush, constantly running from one place to another, speaking fast, and trying to accomplish as much as possible in the shortest amount of time. At times, she requires the High Priestess to step up and stand out. The High Priestess talks quietly, speaks slowly and purposefully, and slows down her movements. This is what makes her a queen, and sets her apart from the rest.

When she enters a room, heads turn, and people listen. Her presence alone commands attention. She doesn't need to raise her voice to be heard, she speaks with a quiet confidence that makes everyone lean in to hear what she has to say. When she speaks, every word is carefully chosen, and each sentence is delivered with intention. Her slow, purposeful speech is a reflection of her inner calmness and wisdom. She knows that rushing through life doesn't lead to success, but rather to burnout and stress.

She takes her time, moves with intention, and trusts that everything will fall into place. Her slow, deliberate movements also reflect her grace and poise. When she walks, she glides, making every step look effortless. She doesn't rush from one place to another, but rather moves with intention, never wasting a single movement.

As she moves and speaks, she exudes a sense of power that comes from deep within. Her quiet demeanor and purposeful actions make her stand out in a world where everyone is in a rush. She knows that true power comes not from speed and busyness, but from inner stillness and focus. The High Priestess understands that there is power in stillness and retreat. She knows that in order to lead, she must take care of herself first. That is why she talks quietly and engages in slow, rhythmic movements like swaying to music or gentle yoga. These practices allow her to quiet her mind and connect with her inner wisdom.

When conflict arises, the High Priestess does not engage in battles. Instead, she knows when to retreat from the situation and take time to revive her spirit. This retreat is not a sign of weakness, but rather a display of strength. By taking time to care for herself, the High Priestess becomes even stronger and more powerful. During this retreat, the High Priestess delays decision-making. She knows that in order to make the best decision, she must be in a calm and centered state of mind. She trusts that when she emerges from her gentle retreat, she will know exactly what to do. When the High Priestess does speak, she chooses her words carefully. She speaks with kindness and gentleness, yet her words are powerful. Her actions are also gentle, yet impactful.

There is power in slowing things down. I am not suggesting you go through every moment of your life in slow motion because that is impossible. And honestly, it would probably be annoying to most people and you would not get much done. However, when you get centered and you draw on your strength from within, you become much more effective in everything you do and there still is a sense of slowing down time. There is an incredible scene in "The Matrix" where Neo, the character played by Keanu Reeves, is getting shot at and bullets are whizzing by him. Time slows down as he dodges the bullets, seeing them clearly as he elegantly and purposefully moves from left to right in slow motion. Time has slowed down for him. This gives him the ability to respond rather than react. He is going to where he needs to be, avoiding danger. Just like Wayne Gretzky, when you are in your power, your level of awareness expands and you can anticipate and respond accordingly. You are never going to get what or where you want by chasing or running away. Being centered gives you power.

To support your inner calm, to bring in the High Priestess, paint your aura with a stunning vibrant gold color. Meditate with this color. By doing so, you will notice your heart rate and breathing become quieter.

In today's fast-paced world, it's easy to get caught up in the chaos and the noise. However, by taking a page from the High Priestess's book and slowing down, we can become more powerful and effective leaders. We can connect with our inner wisdom and make decisions from a place of calm and centeredness. So, the next time you find yourself rushing through life, take a moment to slow down and observe your inner High Priestess. Learn from her example and allow yourself to be present in the moment. Speak slowly and purposefully, move with intention, and trust that everything will fall into place. You too can embody the power and grace of a queen.

FROM THE GROUND UP

The Queen is a woman who exudes power, grace, and strength. She radiates confidence, and nothing seems to shake her. How does she do it? What is the secret to her unwavering composure?

The answer lies in grounding. Grounding is the practice of connecting with the earth, anchoring yourself in the present moment, and centering your energy. For the Queen, grounding is essential. It keeps her rooted in her body and in touch with her inner wisdom.

The Queen is grounded into the earth, grounded into her skin, grounded into her Self. Grounding helps her maintain her strength and power. It makes her immovable and unshakeable. Her soul is anchored into her body making her able to move mountains. Grounding allows her to channel her higher Self in through the body that can take the required action. Anchoring also allows her a channel by which to release the stress, anxiety and tension that comes at her throughout the day so she is not affected by it. It allows you to be energetically connected to your body, in the present moment and be in your authentic self.

The Queen knows that grounding is the key to staying balanced and in control. By staying connected to the earth, she can release any negative energy that comes her way, and stay firmly rooted in her own power.

Grounding is simply the act of connecting with the earth. This can be done by walking barefoot on the grass, sitting with your back against a tree, or even just visualizing roots growing from your feet into the earth.

Grounding allows the Queen to be fully present in the moment. She can tap into her intuition and inner guidance, making decisions that are aligned with her true purpose. She can navigate the world with ease and grace, unshaken by the storms that come her way.

QUIET TIME

To connect with the deepest core of who you are as a woman, you must first get quiet. In our busy, noisy world, it's easy to drown out our internal chatter with distractions like TV, social media, and constant stimulation. But when you finally turn off the noise, you may be surprised by the chatter you hear in your mind.

It can be uncomfortable at first, but trust me, that chatter has always been there. You've just been ignoring it. It's like being in a hotel room with the TV on. You're so focused on the programming that you don't notice the other noises around you. But as soon as you turn off the TV, you hear everything from the couple next door to the baby down the hall.

The same is true for your mind. Once you quiet the external noise, you'll start to hear the internal chatter. It may feel overwhelming, but don't be scared. It's always been there. The key is to be patient with yourself and allow yourself the time and space to listen.

As someone who has taught and practiced a wide range of meditation and intuition techniques, I can tell you that any form of meditation, any practice that helps you get quiet and centered, will help you access your core. It's a powerful and necessary tool for any woman who wants to connect with her deepest self.

As you spend more time in that peaceful space, the noise in your mind will start to dissipate. You'll be able to quiet your thoughts more quickly, and there will be less of a struggle for dominance. The chatter seems to grow louder because it finally has the opportunity to be heard. But don't worry, simply let it pass and return to the stillness. It's almost as if the mind is a child craving attention. Once you give it some, it quiets down and doesn't need as much. The more you spend time in silence, the more the mind gets the attention it has been craving. It learns to trust that it will be heard and therefore it becomes quieter.

Whenever I feel my high priestess is out of balance, I find ways to sit in silence. Even while driving. I will drive in complete silence. We spend so much time in our cars, the car is a wonderful place to connect with any part you desire. When I need my Playmate, my energy kicked up a notch, I play great music. I play it loud, I sing and I do a little dance in the car. When I need to access my CEO, I play educational tapes, lectures, audio books, and other audibles that stimulate me intellectually. When I want to activate my Mother, I play soft, beautiful, gentle songs that are very nurturing and tell a story about life. Love songs, classical and symphonic music all help me connect with my Mother energy. And when I need to activate my High Priestess, I drive in absolute silence.

I highly encourage you to spend one day a week in silence. Now I know for some of us, it might be impossible because we have family or young children, but whatever period of time you can devote, even if it is a half a day, spend it in silence. I'm not suggesting you make a big fanfare over it, wearing a sign that says don't talk to me, I'm in silence. But you can let your family know you will be taking this time for yourself. You can go for a long walk, grab a cup of coffee and sit on a park bench enjoying the sounds of the leaves rustling with the wind. You can simply meander around your town or even spend the day at home in silence. Maya Angelou writes a great short story on "My day away". She spends one day just meandering, no plan, no agenda, no goal. She is focused on her inner voice, and wherever her inner voice wants her to go, she goes.

I have a new client who is really out of balance with her High Priestess, so I had her cut out any source of media for a week. I invited her to come home to no TV, no music and no source of audio, even programs or educational material. She came back the next week and described how difficult it was at first but by the end of the week, felt completely relaxed. She even slept through the night and woke up refreshed and renewed, whereas before, she had numerous sleepless nights.

I invite you to try this at home. Whether you are cooking, cleaning, or getting yourself to bed, do it in silence. Anything except listening to outside voices. Reading is okay, because you are still in your thoughts, but not listening to anything.

BREATHE DARLING

The Queen is never out of breath. She does not take quick shallow breaths. She breathes; slowly and deeply. Taking deep, long, slow breaths are important to your body, your mind and your spirit. Breathing is the life that comes through you. We know the mind controls the body, but it is the breath that controls the mind. Taking that time to breathe throughout the day, full, deep, cleansing and nourishing breaths, connects you to your inner High Priestess. You may notice, if you start paying attention, that you go through your day with shallow breaths. Most people don't breathe. When you are stressed and anxious or running around, and you finally get that moment where you could sit down, what do you want to do? You let out a sigh. There is power in that sigh. You have been holding your breath throughout the day. Taking a purposeful breath, a long, deep inhale followed by a long, deep exhale can decrease your heart rate, your blood pressure, your stress, and get you connected into the core of your being. It gives you access to your truth and your power so you get back in the driver's seat of your life.

Begin a practice of reminding yourself to breathe. A great practice is to anchor it to something you know you will do regularly. You can tell yourself that every time you pull into your driveway, before you enter your home, you will take a deep breath. Every time you are at a red light, just take one deep, long breath. Just notice that red light and program yourself. You see that red light, you take a long, deep breath.

There is a powerful scene in Superman where Clark Kent turns into Superman. He takes his hands and grabs the inside of his shirt. And what you see is, as he is ripping his shirt open, he takes a breath. His chest expands, his shoulders open up, he stands taller and all of a sudden the power just comes through him. That is the power of the breath. It centers us. It makes us strong. It lifts up your energy. That is how we want to be throughout our day. Take those deep powerful breaths, and notice how much power that gives you.

As strange as it sounds, I am going to encourage you to breathe. Commit to one week and try it. Decide on a regular time to take those deep breaths this week. Gift that to yourself. Whether it is at a red light, every time you sit at your computer or office chair, when you put the key in the ignition or take it out, take one long deep breath in and let it out slowly. You will notice an immediate change in your state. If you are heading into a meeting, are going to have a conversation with somebody that makes you a little nervous, about to begin a new project or even send a project off, take a breath. And then go do what you need to do. Notice how quickly that shifts your energy. Notice how much more centered and prepared you feel.

Twenty-six

QUIET STRENGTH

"The power of a woman's quiet strength is often underestimated, but it is what sustains her through the toughest of times and propels her to greatness in the moments that matter most."

ELEGANCE

The Queen has an elegance about her, a knowingness, that is strong, steady and contented. Nothing gets by her. Her strength, albeit quiet strength, is palpable. She need only glance in a certain direction and her court knows how to please her. Her message is clear and she is never questioned for she is the direct link to the most powerful, the king, the holy, the divine.

As women, we are often told to dress and behave in certain ways to be considered "elegant" or "ladylike." But true elegance is much more than surface-level appearances. It's a state of being that emanates from within, a regal grace that is cultivated over time. To embody elegance like a queen, start by cultivating a sense of self-awareness. Take time to reflect on your values, your strengths, and your weaknesses. When you know who you are and what you stand for, you can carry yourself with more confidence and poise.

When it comes to dressing elegantly, quality over quantity is key. Invest in classic, timeless pieces that flatter your figure and make you feel beautiful. Choose fabrics that feel luxurious against your skin and accessories that add a touch of sophistication to any outfit. But elegance isn't just about how you look - it's about how you behave. Queens are known for their grace under pressure, their ability to remain calm and collected in even the most challenging situations. The practice of mindfulness and self-care will help you stay centered and grounded, even in the midst of chaos.

CROWN YOURSELF

The High Priestess is confident and powerful in her own skin. One way to channel your inner Queen and exude that sense of royalty is through the simple act of standing tall, like a ballerina or a queen wearing her crown. Queens wear crowns because it puts them closer to the heavens. Queens wear crowns with pride. You can wear a crown literally or metaphorically. You can wear a metaphorical one by carrying yourself with a regal bearing connecting you to source above. As my ballet instructor used to say, stand straight and lift your head up, imagining a string attached to the top of your head pulling you up towards the heavens. This is not about lifting your nose at people or being arrogant, but rather lifting your head up from your center, radiating confidence and grace.

Posture and body language are crucial in embodying the Queen within. Queens carry themselves with their shoulders back, heads held high, and a regal bearing. Practice good posture, observe how it changes the way you feel and the way others perceive you, and make it a habit. As you step into your power, standing tall and exuding confidence, you'll find that people treat you differently and that you're able to accomplish more than you ever thought possible.

Focus on elongating your body, as clothing that elongates the body is always more flattering on women. For many, heels can create the feeling of royalty and elegance, forcing you to elongate your body and stand straight. A favorite accessory for many women, it can actually serve as a tool to help achieve this statuesque posture and graceful appearance, in addition to wearing the right clothing and accessories.

REIGNING CONFIDENCE

Confidence is often thought of as something that needs to be achieved or acquired through external means, like a new outfit or a promotion at work. Competence creates confidence in the CEO. The CEO is confident because of what she is able to do and accomplish as well as her collection of badges, awards and certificates. The CEO knows her strengths and has talent, skill and ability. She knows she can handle life's situations which lends itself to self-reliance.

Confidence within the High Priestess is innate. Her confidence emerges from her self-assuredness and positive self-concept. Not knowing this distinction creates the imposter syndrome so many smart, capable women suffer from. She feels as if she is an imposter because she relies heavily on her ability to do something for her confidence. On a deep level, she knows that can change, there will be others better than her and she may lose her drive or her abilities at any moment. She does not understand that her brilliance comes from deep within her and is unshakable. She can access it at any time. When a woman relies on her creativity yet does not know where it comes from, she wakes up each day with the debilitating fear that today, it may not come. That feels like death.

When you know who you are, your strengths and weaknesses, your values and beliefs, you develop a strong sense of self. You become comfortable in your own skin, and you radiate that confidence to the world. To tap into your innate confidence, start by exploring yourself. Write down your thoughts, feelings, and experiences, and reflect on them regularly.

No one is perfect, and that's okay. In fact, it's our imperfections that make us unique and special. Instead of trying to hide or fix your flaws, embrace them. Don't compare yourself to others. I have rarely found someone who matched up equally to another and a Queen knows that is a losing battle. Accept that you are not perfect and that's okay. When you stop striving for perfection, you free yourself to be yourself. You become more authentic, and that authenticity is what makes you confident.

Confidence also comes from trusting yourself. When you believe in your abilities, your decisions, and your choices, you radiate confidence. To tap into your innate confidence, start by trusting yourself. Make decisions that align with your values and beliefs, and stand by them. When you trust yourself, others will trust you too.

Confidence can also be influenced by the people and environments around you. Surround yourself with positivity. Spend time with people who uplift you, and avoid those who bring you down. Create an environment that supports your growth and well-being. When you surround yourself with positivity, you feel more confident and optimistic. Your confidence is already within you, waiting to be unleashed. Allow her to shine.

I AM

The two most powerful words in the English language are "I Am." What comes after those two words can shape your reality and determine your destiny. The power of "I Am" is not just a mere utterance, it is a declaration of your identity and a proclamation of your intent. These words have the ability to transform lives for it declares your existence. Whatever follows 'I Am' will come looking for you. This means that whatever you declare after those two words will manifest itself in your life. If you declare that you are strong, resilient, and confident, those qualities will start showing up in your life.

By declaring "I am" statements that affirm our greatness, we are stepping into our power and claiming our birthright. What follows those two words is a reflection of our beliefs and intentions. Therefore, it's crucial to be intentional about our "I am" statements and declare those that empower and uplift us. So, what are your "I am" statements? Are they empowering or limiting? Do you often say I am brilliant, smart, beautiful? Or do you catch yourself saying I'm an idiot, broke or unhappy? Remember, whatever follows "I am" will come looking for you, so choose wisely. Use the power of "I am" to affirm your identity, claim your power, and manifest your desires.

Set your powerful "I AM" statements or intentions daily at minimum. Your intention could be, I am powerful, I am centered, I am caring, I am nurturing or I am love. If you were to step into the best, highest version of you in this moment, who would you need to be? Then write that down in the morning. Write "I am…" then fill in the blank. Then bring that intention into your day. Notice how much of that quality you can bring into your experience throughout your day. If I say, I am passionate, loving and purposeful, then I notice throughout the day, how many more times I bring love, passion and purpose into my experience. What would I be doing or saying knowing I am love, purpose and passion. I am grounding who I am meant to be in every moment of my day and becoming more of my greatest, highest self.

TAKING A BREAK FROM DATING

There was a period of time when I was dating a number of men and decided it was time for me to be alone, to focus on me. I am sure I am the only one that has ever been in that situation. I would like to say I was surrendering to what the divine had in store for me, trusting that the right man was out there if I just stopped looking. In all honesty, it was more of a resignation. I was tired of the incessant self doubts and dating drama; I was hurt that the men I was dating were not stepping up. No one wanted me, not the men I wanted at least, and none of them were confessing their undying love. I was working too hard and getting exhausted in the interim. The sleepless nights, the confusion, the incessant mind reading attempts trying to justify bad behavior thinking "but he must like me even though I don't hear from him for days on end".

I decided I needed to be single, at least for a while. Three months I gave myself. That is a perfect cycle where big shifts and transformations can occur. Following the forced resignation from the drama-filled life of dating, did I mention most of it was online, I finally surrendered to singledom.

I was no longer fighting it, no longer regretting being alone and wishing for a different situation or life. I surrendered to what was in store for me. This was an opportunity for me to go inward. Instead of trying to fill the void, I used my loneliness to learn to stand firm, to find my inner strength, to equip myself to be a woman of courage, of truth and of dignity. This was a season of my life where I was alone. Rather than feeling lonely, I began to focus on myself without distraction.

I learned what would make me fall in love with me rather than focus on what would make him fall in love with me. This time was for me, to find the incredible truth of my soul, my essence, the spirit inside of me. Instead of being a time of passive and futile waiting, it was a beautiful and exciting time for me to go on an inward adventure of self-discovery, fulfillment and becoming the woman I love, the woman of my dreams.

So many smart, beautiful, incredible women are single because the dating world has changed so much. In addition, the dynamics between men and women are broken, rules have shifted, and poor behavior on the parts of both men and women are rampant, which is partly what this book is attempting to remedy. The High Priestess knows how to step back, focus on herself and connect with her love for herself. She closes off the all-access door which, when she is ready, only allows her true King to come in. And most importantly, she knows how to differentiate the King from the boy.

RAISING THE BAR

The High Priestess holds herself to very high standards and expects nothing less than greatness from herself, including full authenticity and integrity. She also holds those around her to similarly high standards, but not in a nagging (unbalanced Mother) or bossy (unbalanced CEO) manner. She never approaches others with a message of "you're not enough", instead, she sees the greatness and brilliance in those around her, even beyond what they see in themselves. By only seeing their potential, the High Priestess allows others to see themselves in a positive light. She believes in them so much, they start to believe in themselves.

Every man wants a woman who is going to make him aspire to something more than he is. With the man in your life, we do not come from a motherly place of "you need to get your shtuff together". She does not Mother him by reprimanding him. We expect them to do the right thing. And when they fall below that, we let them know in subtle ways that this is not okay with me. Never making them wrong and also not pointing out when they make a mistake. The High Priestess knows no one is perfect and mistakes are part of learning. She expects the best and gives room for him to grow into his greatness. If it does not affect her negatively, she can ignore his mistake or simply not bring any attention to it. She also is sure to reward him when he is stepping up. She is able to provide him support and lend him her belief when needed. A man thrives on being with a woman who believes in him.

A friend of mine is a very successful speaker trainer, author, and coach. He travels often and is doing some amazing things in the world. He immigrated from Iran to Canada with his wife, a dream and limited cash to start this business. He struggled for a year to get anything off the ground. Near the end of the year, their eleventh month, they had $2,000 left and there was no money about to come. They had nothing in the pipeline. He kept trying to build his business and things were not happening as quickly as he needed. He was stressed carrying the heavy burden and the weight that was on his shoulders. He didn't know what to do and felt like a failure. He sat his wife down and said, honey, we have $2,000 left. This can either pay for one month's rent, but after that, we have nothing. Or it can pay for a flight home. The difficult choice was to stay and then they would be broke, probably even homeless after one month, or they can just go back to their old life and give up on their dream. And what she said brings tears to my eyes every time I share this. She asked him, have we ever given up on our dreams before? He said No. And then she said, why would we do that now?

This was just such a beautiful gift to him because he didn't know how he was going to do it, yet she believed in him. She wasn't doing it for him. But she held him to such a high standard, believing that he could figure it out, and she was willing to stand by his side as he did just that. She was willing to go down on that ship with him because she trusted him. That is what a man needs and desires. This is what inspires a man to step up. He is the most devoted husband to her, has a great heart, always remembering where he came from and the struggles. He remembers that she is the one that lifts him on a daily basis. She is the one that believes in him. Women can bring so much beautiful power in a relationship and in turn inspire devotion from her man.

By the same token, the High Priestess is not afraid to tell him when he is underperforming. But at the end of the day, she believes in him. She is the ultimate teammate. Everything we do as women should be encouraging people around us to be a better person. That includes our husbands or boyfriends, our children, and the people that work for us.

I was once at a baseball tournament. I was dating a man who coached, so I often accompanied him on his trips. We were in the hallway of a hotel, the coaches standing around in a circle discussing the kids and the games. One of the coaches' fiancés and I were listening in. The men began to go over the wins of the recent games. How Bobby did a great job backing up the second baseman and how they appreciated how well the pitcher and catcher communicated throughout the weekend. At one point, Kimberly turned to her fiancé and said "I appreciate you". All the men turned to her perplexed. It was straight out of left field. Seeing the puzzled look on her face, she went on, I thought we were appreciating each other and I just wanted you to know how much I appreciate you. He didn't say a thing, both embarrassed and proud yet pulled her closer to him. It was a sweet poignant moment that silently made him feel powerful.

I am often saddened at gatherings where spouses stand around in a circle bad mouthing each other. Airing their dirty laundry and making fun of their husband or wife's bad habits all for a few laughs or worse, to get people to side with them to see the faults of their significant other.

The most beautiful gift a Queen can give her man is to boast about him in front of others. Share what you love about him. Talk about his great qualities. Let others know the amazing things he does. Even if he isn't around to hear, it will get around to him. He will want to raise his own standards, to shine, to be better and to be the King you want him to be.

When I was young, I watched "As good as it gets" with Jack Nicholson who played Melvin and Helen Hunt who played Connelly. Melvin is a jerk and rude to everyone he meets. He takes Connelly to dinner and after flippantly insulting her, she threatens to walk out and demands that he pay her a compliment to undo the insult. After some hemming and hawing, he finally says "You make me want to be a better man". She was taken aback and said "That's the best compliment anyone has ever given me". I'm thinking "What???" That wasn't a compliment at all. That has nothing to do with her. I was yelling at him in my head, Melvin, this isn't about you, this is about her, pay her a real compliment. As I have matured and gotten in touch with my own inner Queen, I realized it was a great compliment because what he was acknowledging is that she was a Queen and she held him to a high standard. He in turn felt powerful, strong and stepped up into his inner King.

Women in their power have the ability to positively influence all those around her. The High Priestess is the one that inspires others to raise their game in all areas of life. You can lift up the vibration of others by being encouraging and by looking for the best in everyone. Even with people who are not necessarily acting great in the moment, or making the best choices, she is able to bring out the best in that person, regardless. She gently pushes them towards being higher versions of themselves, and holding high expectations for them.

The Queen always leaves others better than she found them. You carry the high vibration which will naturally emanate from you. You can walk into an absolute pitch black room and all it takes is lighting a single match to illuminate the room. You hold that light and even if there is darkness around you, you don't succumb to it. You stand steady and strong holding that light. You can become that light. You are the light.

ALWAYS BE KIND

The High Priestess treats everyone with respect. She remembers her manners in every situation, unless of course the CEO has to step in to protect her boundaries. She is graceful, does not raise her voice and is a lady in every sense of the word. Embodying the timeless elegance of a true queen is about kindness and compassion. Treat others with respect and generosity, and you will radiate a warmth and grace that is truly regal. The power in the High Priestess is to be kind and compassionate, to lead by example and create a world that is filled with love and understanding.

The truth is, kindness is not just a virtue, it is a superpower. When we approach others with kindness, we open doors and build bridges that might otherwise have remained closed. We create connections and find common ground, even with people who might seem vastly different from ourselves. And perhaps most importantly, we inspire others to do the same.

But being kind is not always easy. It can be hard to extend compassion to people who have hurt us, or to people whose beliefs and values differ from our own. It requires a level of vulnerability and openness that can feel uncomfortable or even scary. It means setting healthy boundaries, communicating clearly and respectfully, and standing up for ourselves and our values. The High Priestess knows this and is strong enough to rise above it. As the Dalai Llama shared, there are friends and there are sacred friends. Sacred friends are those that are tough to love, the ones that can annoy, hurt or disappoint us. The CEO knows how to protect you from being hurt while the High Priestess knows how to use these opportunities as a way to cultivate even more compassion, love, and wisdom.

There are many ways to show kindness and It can start with small acts of love and understanding. It can be as simple as smiling at a stranger, holding the door open for someone, or taking the time to listen to a friend who is going through a tough time. It means being present and engaged, and putting aside our own judgments and biases to truly see and hear the people around us.

Being kind also means being brave. It means standing up for what is right, even when it's hard. It means using our voices and our platforms to speak out against injustice, and to advocate for those who are marginalized or oppressed. Being regal, kind and compassionate is a way of being in the world that can bring us closer to ourselves, to others, and to a greater sense of purpose. When we choose kindness, we tap into a deep well of inner strength and resilience that can carry us through even the toughest of times.

MORAL COMPASS

"Be the change you wish to see in the world"
~ Mahatma Gandhi ~

The High Priestess is the moral compass within any relationship, organization or institution. She holds high values and upholds standards for others to follow. She consistently makes choices based on her values, beliefs, and principles. She is a person who lives with integrity and inspires others to do the same. Whether she is in a relationship, organization, or institution, she is a beacon of light, shining the way towards what is right and just.

She is not afraid to stand up for what she believes in, even if it means going against the status quo. She has a strong sense of self and is guided by her inner compass. She is not swayed by external influences or the opinions of others. Instead, she listens to her heart and follows the path that feels true to her.

As the moral compass, the High Priestess sets the tone for the environment around her. She creates a culture of honesty, trust, and respect. Her actions and words are consistent, and people can rely on her to be truthful and transparent. She encourages others to do the same, in fact requires it, creating a community of people who share common values and beliefs.

In her love life, she sets clear boundaries and expectations for her partner. She communicates her values, priorities, and non-negotiables early on in the relationship, so there are no misunderstandings or surprises later on. For example, she might say, "I value honesty and communication in a relationship. If there are any issues, I want us to talk about them openly and respectfully." In the workplace, she doesn't cut corners or compromise her values for the sake of success or advancement. She treats everyone with respect and kindness, regardless of their position or status. She holds herself accountable for her actions and takes responsibility for any mistakes or missteps. With her family, she is a role model for her children, siblings, and extended family members. She teaches them important values such as kindness, respect, honesty, and responsibility by living them herself. She provides a listening ear and offers wise advice when needed. She sets clear boundaries and expectations for behavior, and she holds family members accountable when they violate them.

The High Priestess lives her life with intention and purpose. She leads by example, showing others what it means to live a life of purpose and meaning. She inspires others to be their best selves and to strive for greatness. She recognizes the importance of her actions and their impact on others. She strives to make the world a better place by embodying the values she holds dear and inspiring others to do the same. Her presence is felt, and her impact is significant.

Twenty-seven

TRUE POWER

"True power is not about competing with others but about staying true to yourself, your values, and your integrity. When you tap into this inner strength, you will find that there is no need to compete because you are already more than enough."

COMPETITION

The High Priestess knows there is no need to compete with other people, especially women. Men, on the other hand, are designed for competition. They are the competitive species. Competition was critical for survival as men needed to stake their territory. Men fight with their fists, knives or guns. They know the rules. They understand that if one is challenged, the other has to meet that challenge or fear seeming weak, cowardly or lacking in confidence. Weakness can mean death for a man. For men, it is not personal. Women on the other hand look at competition as a personal attack. This is because women are designed for community, for holding people together and for creating peace among groups. For this reason, in competition, women are going against their nature. When forced to fight, they do it in covert ways. While men have their knives out, women keep their knives hidden in their purse. Women can be brutal to each other and hold onto grudges and resentment, long after a fight, win or lose.

There were many fights I broke up while working at an inner city high school. I never hesitated to get between big boys, even football players weighing over 200 pounds. The sight of a woman, me, wearing heels and a skirt, demanding that they stop in my high pitched female voice seemed to immediately stop the fighting. Girls however were fights I always dreaded. It would often take several muscular male staff members to stop a girl fight. These young ladies seemed to go into a rage, completely blacking out and fighting for their life. There was no end in sight for them and no backing down. Even after getting pulled apart, there were persistent signs of aggression, harsh words, threats, and another round of cursing. Women carry their anger and resentment and rarely get over it. The fighting would continue with girlfriends getting involved, talking about each other, backstabbing and sabotaging. These traits carry over to women who know better than to get physical. They gossip, put others down behind their back and sabotage anything they can. Backstabbing is popular among women who are in competition for the same job, man or even status. Women carry their anger, resentment and rarely get over it.

In contrast, when men fight, win or lose, they move on. They shake hands, appreciate the challenge and funny enough, can even be friends afterwards. Men compete to bring each other up, to level up their game. A man who plays basketball would rather have a one-on-one match with a Michael Jordan versus a high school amateur. Even though they know they are going to lose pretty badly, they play with the more competent player because they know it will raise their own game. They invite the challenge to elevate their own level.

Women avoid confrontation. The fear of standing up to a person comes from the lack of the CEO energy. They are threatened by other women and tend to cut each other down. When other women win, she feels there is less for her. The High Priestess sees beyond that and lifts other women up. She knows there is a power within her that is the source of all she desires. She embodies this truth and knows there is no lack of jobs, promotions, men or resources. She is able to access the resourceful within herself and knows how to meet all her needs and go after what she wants. The High Priestess is never threatened by others. She understands that what others do and what they accomplish does not diminish her value. It does not diminish her sense of self-worth. She is able to lift up people around her. She does not gossip. There is no need for it for she values each person with all their uniqueness and flaws. She does not talk bad about others. She treats everyone with the utmost respect and no one is exempt from her kindness.

The High Priestess rises to the top on her own accord, not on the backs of others. Competition is vital to gain awareness of one's level, to up level your skills and to stretch you beyond your comfort zone. Ambition is a critical and healthy trait that allows us to evolve as a species. Learn the traits that lead to success and those that lead to failure. Commit to constant and never ending self improvement and continue to reach for higher quality in everything you are and do.

KNOW THYSELF

The High Priestess participates in reflecting on her Self and her life. Self-inquiry is the process of knowing: knowing oneself, connecting to your higher self and evolving as an aware conscious woman. Self-inquiry is continuing to look in the mirror, asking empowering questions that allow you to harness the opportunities, gifts and blessings in life regardless of how they look on the outside.

This is an ongoing process of reflection, introspection, and self-awareness. It is a powerful tool that allows you to deepen your understanding of who you are, what you believe, and what you want out of life. Through self-inquiry, you can uncover the limiting beliefs and negative patterns that hold you back and cultivate a deeper sense of inner peace and fulfillment.

Many women are conditioned to prioritize the needs of others above their own, often at the expense of their own well-being. Self-inquiry offers a path for women to reclaim their power, by connecting to their inner selves and cultivating a deeper sense of self-awareness. By asking questions such as "Who am I?" and "What do I really want?", women can gain insight into their true desires and begin to take steps towards creating a life that aligns with their authentic selves.

Self-inquiry also helps women to identify and challenge the limiting beliefs and negative self-talk that often hold them back. By shining a light on these inner voices, women can begin to reframe their thoughts and beliefs, and cultivate a more positive and empowering mindset which can lead to greater self-confidence, resilience, and a sense of purpose and direction in life.

Practicing self-inquiry can take many forms, from journaling and meditation to seeking the guidance of a coach or therapist. Whatever form it takes, the key is to approach the process with openness, curiosity, and a willingness to explore and embrace all aspects of yourself. By engaging in this ongoing process of self-discovery, you can deepen your connection to your higher self and tap into the infinite potential that lies within.

Self-inquiry is a journey, not a destination, and it requires patience, commitment, and self-compassion. But the rewards are immeasurable. By taking the time to know and understand yourself on a deeper level, you can transform your life from the inside out, and become the empowered, conscious Queen you were always meant to be.

INTEGRITY

"Integrity is doing the right thing, even when no one is watching"
~ C.S. Lewis ~

The High Priestess possesses unwavering conviction in her beliefs, values, and integrity, holding steadfast to her high ideals and what she holds to be true. She knows her values. She knows her beliefs and what keeps her in alignment with her truth. She is authentic. Authenticity is not a cookie cutter image of everyone else. Authenticity means being in full alignment, body, mind and soul. Authenticity is when your identity, beliefs, attitude, behavior, and actions are all in alignment. If I say my highest value is honesty, then my actions consistently reflect that. My beliefs and attitude always reflect that I am an honest person. and I attract honest people.

The High Priestess embodies unshakable conviction in her beliefs and values, standing resolute in their defense. Her unwavering commitment to these principles is not expressed through aggressive confrontation, but through her very presence. In her steadfastness, she demonstrates a quiet strength that commands respect and admiration.

Unlike the traditional image of a CEO fighting tooth and nail to achieve their goals, the High Priestess' fight is one of being fully present and grounded. She holds her ground with a sense of inner calm, radiating an energy that is palpable to all those around her. Her steadfastness is not rooted in stubbornness, but rather in a deep understanding of herself and her values.

The High Priestess' presence is an anchor in a world of shifting values and moral ambiguity. In her presence, others feel a sense of safety and security, knowing that they are in the company of someone who holds true to their convictions. It is through this unwavering commitment to what she believes that the High Priestess inspires those around her to do the same.

In a society that often values compromise over conviction, the High Priestess is a beacon of hope for those seeking to stay true to themselves and their beliefs. Her unwavering presence serves as a reminder that sometimes the most powerful form of resistance is simply standing firm in one's truth.

The story of a slender unassuming man carrying grocery bags who blocked a line of tanks on June 5, 1989, in Beijing is a powerful example of the strength of conviction and standing up for what one believes in, even in the face of opposition. The Tank Man, as he is called, stood in front of a row of tanks during the Chinese military's violent crackdown on pro-democracy protesters in Tiananmen Square, blocking their ability to progress into the crowd.

The Tank Man's actions were a powerful symbol of resistance and a reminder of the individual's ability to stand up to power. In a similar way, the High Priestess embodies the same spirit of conviction and unwavering dedication to her beliefs and values. She is unshakable and unmovable in the face of opposition and adversity. Just like the Tank Man, the High Priestess doesn't use force or aggression to make her point, but rather her presence and inner strength. Her steadfastness and unyielding commitment to her values inspire those around her to stand up for their own beliefs and convictions.

The High Priestess possesses a powerful presence that goes beyond words. She does not need to struggle or fight to make a point. Her conviction and strength come from within, and they emanate from her being. This presence is so powerful that it can stop a war.

This story serves as a powerful reminder that we can all make a difference in the world by standing up for what we believe in, even when it's hard, and that one person's actions can have a powerful impact on the world around them. The High Priestess is a reminder of the same message, embodying the spirit of strength and conviction that we can all strive for in our own lives.

LITTLE VOICE

As a teacher of intuition, I am often asked how to develop intuition. Most people are aware of their intuition on some level. They get intuitive hits about life, yet few are so connected to it that they follow their internal guidance system. Everyone is psychic. I prefer not to use that word because there is such a negative connotation or charge on it in society, but in reality, everyone has an inner voice that knows what they should do, where they should go, what they should say and to whom. This internal voice and guidance system can be cultivated by going into the silence. In the silence, connecting to your inner knowing is easier because you are able to clear out the outer noise, conflict and chaos. Throughout our day, we are constantly being bombarded with noise: physical noise, other people's expectations, thoughts and programming through the media and the problems of the world, our community and even in our home. Cultivating that silence allows us to block out the noise so we can connect on a deep level in order to access our truth.

Developing her intuition is of high importance to the Queen. For a woman to be in her power, she has to be in her truth. The Queen is directed and guided by her internal truth. She is required to have a direct line to her truth.

When you look at life's problems or circumstances that can be devastating to anyone, accessing her truth would have and will avoid the negative pitfalls of those experiences. Take a minute to look back at your life right now. Perhaps you had a health issue, maybe your husband cheated on you or left you, perhaps you found out one of your children was addicted to substances, or maybe you discovered a co-worker was sabotaging you behind your back. If you were to truly be honest with yourself, would you not agree that on some level, you knew. Your husband began shutting off his phone and you had an inkling something was up, but were too afraid to ask or admit anything was wrong. You chalked off your child's rebellion as just being a teenager, but your gut kept you worried that there might be something deeper. You felt yucky every time your co-worker gave you a smile that you somehow knew was fake, but ignored it because you so wanted to be liked.

We are given messages all the time, sometimes we listen to them, like the time you didn't quite feel right and went to the doctor, and sometimes you don't, like the stories we hear of someone who had been living with slight discomfort for years, ignoring it, until they finally got diagnosed with stage 4 cancer.

The High Priestess never ignores her intuition, and if something is off, she honors and trusts herself and the information she is getting. Then she allows the CEO to step in and take action, whether it be to confront someone, make an appointment with the doctor, or leave a relationship. She knows that by honoring and trusting herself, she can avoid negative pitfalls and live a life in alignment with her truth.

VISION

The High Priestess reigns supreme as a visionary. She is the mastermind behind the big picture, the one who is in touch with infinite possibilities and the wellspring of innovation. She has access to a labyrinth of new ideas and creativity, all bubbling beneath the surface, waiting to be unleashed. But what sets the High Priestess apart from the rest is her ability to access ideas that have never been brought up before. She brings forth a kind of creativity that is beyond the Playmate's creative spark. Her visions are not limited by what has already been done or what is currently possible. Instead, she taps into a well of inspiration from the Universe that is boundless and ever-flowing, allowing her to materialize ideas that have never before seen the light of day.

All great change requires a Visionary to lead the way and a CEO to implement the movement. Great leaders are often celebrated for their vision and inspiration, and behind every successful visionary, there is a CEO. The High Priestess understands the importance of having a strong team that balances both visionary ideas and practical implementation.

When we look back at some of the greatest visionaries in history, we can see that they always had someone who was able to take their ideas and turn them into a reality. Walt Disney, for example, was a visionary who dreamed up fantastical worlds and characters that captured the hearts of millions. And it was his brother Roy who managed the finances, secured loans, and ensured the business was running smoothly. Without Roy's steady hand, Walt Disney's creative empire would have never taken off.

Similarly, Steve Jobs, the co-founder of Apple, was known for his innovative ideas that revolutionized the technology industry. It was Steve Wozniak, his college friend and co-founder, who helped turn those ideas into tangible products that consumers could use.

Martin Luther King moved hundreds of thousands of people to create a movement that changed our planet, changed the country, and brought civil rights to our nation. Even Martin Luther King Jr., a figurehead in the civil rights movement, had Bayard Rustin and Ralph Abernathy working behind the scenes to organize protests, rallies, and marches. They were the ones who ensured that King's vision was executed in a way that had a real impact on society.

The High Priestess understands that having a visionary idea is half the battle. She requires a strong team to support and implement those ideas, otherwise, they will remain just that - ideas. The High Priestess knows that in order to bring your vision to life, you need to surround yourself with people who complement your strengths and weaknesses. When you have a team that is working in harmony, anything is possible.

In the world, the dreamers and the doers are often perceived as two separate entities. We tend to think that if you have a vision, if you have a dream, that it will automatically come true. But that is only part of the equation. Without the CEO, without the practical logic-minded person, that vision will not become a reality, or if it does, it won't last.

This partnership between the visionary and the CEO is what creates greatness. These most iconic visionaries in history, from Walt Disney to Steve Jobs to Martin Luther King Jr., all of them had someone behind them, someone who could take their dreams and turn them into something tangible. Without Roy Disney, Disney would never have become the multi-billion dollar empire it is today. Without Steve Wozniak, the iPhone and other Apple products would not exist. And without Bayard Rustin and Ralph Abernathy, his vision of a more just and equal society would never have been realized.

The reason I emphasize this now is because so many people in this New Age world think that all they have to do is have a vision, have a dream and it will come true. And it is true, yet there has to be that other piece. Unless it is grounded with the CEO energy, it cannot survive or be sustainable. The job of the inner CEO can simply be to find someone who is skilled in specific required tasks or projects. Without that partnership, nothing manifests.

That is how great things are created. The bible states "Without vision, the people perish". Without the visionary, these companies could never have been as big and as life changing as they were. Without vision, there is no evolution. Both are required to create power and purpose. This partnership creates so much more than a product, a service. so much more than an idea, it creates magic.

The High Priestess knows her vision is indeed powerful, and she calls on her inner CEO for the practical, strategic mindset in order to harness that power. The two have the ability to create something truly remarkable. Together, they can achieve more than just a product, a service, or an idea. They can change the world.

Truly, the High Priestess is a master of the creative arts, a visionary whose ideas and innovations will shape the world for generations to come. She is the one who sees beyond the status quo and charts a course towards uncharted territories. She is a trailblazer, a pioneer who partners with her CEO who is not afraid to take risks and venture into unexplored realms. Her creativity is not just beautiful but transformative, changing the very fabric of our understanding of what is possible.

Twenty-eight

HEALING AND GROWING

"Journaling is like whispering to one's self and listening at the same time."
~ Mina Murray ~

GRATITUDE

Gratitude is the key to unlocking the power of the High Priestess within you. Gratitude is the act of acknowledging all of the blessings in your life, both big and small, and recognizing the beauty that surrounds you every day. Gratitude allows you to connect to the present moment and appreciate the richness of life.

Even those who have been practicing personal development for a long time can forget to practice gratitude. It's easy to get caught up in the pursuit of bigger and better things and forget to appreciate what you already have. High Achievers are often looking for the next mountain to climb and the next goal to achieve. With their sights always set in the future, they forget to take a breath, take note of what is in their life in the moment and bless the gifts in their life.

But the High Priestess reminds us to take a moment to be grateful for all the wonderful things in our lives.

The beauty of gratitude is that it multiplies. When you express gratitude, you attract more things to be grateful for. Whatever you appreciate, appreciates. It's a powerful cycle that brings abundance and joy into your life. Whether it's the people in your life, the experiences you've had, or the smallest of things, acknowledging your gratitude for them will bring more of them into your life.

There are many successful people who after having achieved a big goal ask, "now what?" It was such a great accomplishment, everything else pales in comparison. They struggle to find meaning in their life after accomplishing such monumental feats. Some become depressed or turn to alcohol to cope with their inability to find gratitude in the small things.

Being in love with life is what gives us the fuel to continue to pursue our dreams and live our lives with purpose. Gratitude is the bridge that connects us to that love. It allows us to see the beauty in everything and feel a deep connection to the world around us.

So, take a moment each day to acknowledge your gratitude. Focus on the blessings in your life, no matter how small they may seem. Appreciate the people, experiences, and things that bring you joy. By doing so, you will awaken the power of the High Priestess within you and unlock the abundance and happiness that life has to offer.

JOURNALING

When it comes to personal development and self-discovery, there are many powerful tools and practices that can help us get in touch with our core, our essence, our spirit, and our higher self. In this regard, we've talked about meditation, breathing, silence, and now we'll focus on journaling and setting intentions.

Here's some news that may not be new to some, but it's a truth we should all hear: everything we think, say to ourselves, consider saying to others, our habits, and beliefs are not really ours. They are all subconscious programming that we've absorbed since we were babies. To get in touch with our core, our essence, our spirit, and our higher self, we need to let go of this self, this subconscious programming. And journaling is a powerful tool for this because it helps us pay attention to our thoughts.

When we write down our thoughts, we are grounding them, creating clarity in the moment and excavating all the thoughts, feelings, beliefs, and attitudes that we've absorbed. We can then consciously decide what serves us and what doesn't, what is from our core and what is just programming that's been running our lives. Writing down our thoughts is crucial because we can have up to 60,000 thoughts running through our heads, and we may not even be aware of them all. Journaling gives us a chance to begin paying attention to those thoughts and those programs.

Journaling is an avenue to get in touch with our core, because it helps us clear out the noise and the chatter in our mind. It allows us to excavate all of the thoughts, feelings, beliefs, and programming that we have, and to consciously decide what serves us and what doesn't serve us, what's from our core and what's not from our core. Writing down our thoughts helps us ground them and create clarity in the moment. It also allows us to participate in the process of self-inquiry, which can lead to deep insights, revelations, and breakthroughs.

To make the most out of journaling, it's important to set aside some time each day, ideally in the morning or before going to bed, to reflect on your thoughts, feelings, and experiences. You can start by writing down whatever comes to mind, without judging or censoring yourself. Just let the words flow and see where they take you. You can write about your dreams, your fears, your goals, your relationships, your past, your present, or your future. You can also use prompts or questions to guide your writing, such as "What am I grateful for today?", "What do I want to let go of?", "What do I want to invite into my life?", or "What can I learn from this situation?".

When it comes to setting intentions, it's important to be clear, specific, and positive. Instead of focusing on what you don't want or what you're afraid of, focus on what you do want and what you're capable of. Start by deciding who the best, highest version of you is in that moment. It could be someone who is confident, compassionate, creative, courageous, or any other quality that resonates with you. Write that down in your journal and put it after the words "I am". For example, you can write "I am confident and capable of achieving my goals" or "I am kind and loving to myself and others". Make it compelling and easy to read, so that you can remind yourself of it throughout the day.

Remember that journaling and setting intentions are not magic pills or quick fixes. They are ongoing practices that require patience, consistency, and self-reflection. They are also tools that can complement other practices, such as meditation, yoga, therapy, or coaching. The more you use them, the more you'll discover about yourself, and the more you'll be able to align with your core values, your purpose, and your vision. So give them a try, experiment with different approaches, and see what works best for you. You might be surprised by what you uncover. So, to dig deep and connect with our core, we must start by letting go of our subconscious programming. Journaling is a powerful tool to help us achieve this.

FORGIVENESS

Recently, I stumbled upon a reel that left me perplexed. A man was stopped on the street, and the interviewer asked him his age. He was 42. The interviewer followed up with a seemingly harmless question, "what's it like being 42?" His answer saddened me. He said he was tired, it was tough, and difficult being 42 with all of life's challenges. He was only 42, yet he was already carrying so much baggage.

As I watched the reel, I began to reflect on my own life and the older people I know. Although I have met many lovely, vibrant elders, I have also encountered an equal number of old, grumpy men and women. It left me wondering why they get that way. Is it because of the years they have lived, carrying all of their burdens?

Personally, I would love to live to be 150, but I cannot imagine carrying 150 years of baggage - the pain, the betrayals, the heartbreaks, and the failures. It's a lot, and I can understand why some people reach a certain age and say they are ready to die. They are tired and want out of their life. I firmly believe that this tiredness is because of the past and the lack of forgiveness. Holding onto grudges, anger, and emotions over past hurts can and will affect you. Unforgiveness is a tremendous burden to carry, whereas forgiving frees you up, lightens your heart, and gives you a youthful energy of a fresh start every day. That's how I want to live each day of my long, beautiful life. Free of the weight of unforgiveness, I choose to carry only love, gratitude, and a youthful energy in my heart. This is the way of the High Priestess.

I have my clients join my practice of forgiveness every single morning. They ask themselves who they need to forgive and they consciously let that person go. They no longer allow free rent in their mind and in their heart. Ask yourself now, who do you forgive? If you are still living and breathing, there is somebody who still has energy in your space because you are holding on to some grudge, resentment, anger, or bitterness. As Nelson Mandela put it, unforgiveness is like drinking poison expecting the other person to die. This energy is draining and is affecting your ability to move forward and feel whole and complete. It also affects your ability to create for yourself. Say a little silent prayer of forgiveness, send them love and release them.

CHARISMA

Charisma is a mysterious and captivating quality that some people seem to possess effortlessly. It's an elusive quality that's hard to define but impossible to ignore. We often say there's a charisma about someone to describe that intangible something that makes them shine. And the High Priestess, she embodies charisma like no other. It's not just her beauty, though that's undeniable. It's not just her grace, though she moves with a mesmerizing fluidity. It's something deeper, something more profound.

The High Priestess has a charisma that comes from within. It's the light that shines from her character, the strength that radiates from her spirit, and the wisdom that emanates from her soul. She's a woman who knows who she is, what she wants, and where she's going. She is enchanting and enchanted. And that confidence, that self-assurance, is what makes her so enchanting. People are drawn to her like moths to a flame, and they can't help but feel inspired and uplifted in her presence. She has a way of making everyone feel seen and heard, of making everyone feel like they matter.

But the High Priestess isn't just a recipient of admiration and devotion. She's enchanted too, by the beauty of the world around her, by the mysteries that surround her, by the possibilities that lie ahead. She's a woman who's always in awe of the magic of life, and that sense of wonder is what keeps her shining. And so, when we talk about charisma, we're really talking about the High Priestess. She's the embodiment of everything that makes a person magnetic and mesmerizing, and she reminds us that true beauty comes from within.

HIGH PRIESTESS CONCLUSION

The High Priestess is what makes a woman, a lady and a queen. The High Priestess is a force to be reckoned with. She embodies all the traits of a true Queen, emanating power, poise, and confidence with every elegant step she takes. Her aura radiates grace, an inner calm that comes from knowing her own self-worth and never compromising on it. She is connected with her center and with divinity. She goes through life extremely powerful without having to exert force because she knows on a cellular level that she is connected to something extremely powerful, greater than her own physical presence.

The High Priestess is always a lady and is always kind. But when there is danger around and she senses it, then the CEO steps in and takes care of her. The High Priestess can maintain her composure, but the CEO is going to say, not here, not now, you need to leave or I need to leave.

In order to express the High Priestess, create a daily spiritual practice that brings you into conscious awareness. Read motivational material, it could be prayer, a self-help book, or religious material. There is an invisible power within us. This power is your essence, it's your divinity, and when you align to that power, there is nothing you cannot have or be or do.

On an elemental level she uses fire to connect with her spirituality. If you want to get in touch with your High Priestess, spending time around fire allows more of that pure spiritual energy to embody your life. Being in front of a fireplace or fire pit or even lighting a candle will bring in more of that energy.

Her connection to the element of fire only adds to her spirit, igniting her passion and drive to be the best version of herself.

In every situation, the High Priestess chooses to present herself in a way that is both powerful and elegant. Her words are chosen with care, and her point of view is expressed with conviction and poise. She never stoops to negativity or engages in confrontations, instead choosing to handle any situation with the utmost class and grace. Her loyalty to those she cares for is unshakeable, and her kindness is ever-present.

The High Priestess is the epitome of elegance, standing tall and confident in her beliefs and values. She understands that there is no need to put others down or engage in gossip because she has no desire to belittle anyone. Her strength comes from within, and it is this inner strength that allows her to exude a level of grace that is unmatched. She is a true queen, embodying all the traits of grace, power, and elegance. She inspires others through her aura, her energy, and her presence, and serves as a role model for all who aspire to greatness. May we all strive to embody the spirit of the High Priestess and awaken the queen within ourselves.

Ways to get in touch with the High Priestess

- Spend time alone in quiet reflection, meditation or prayer
- Wear clothes that make you feel confident and elegant
- Speak slowly and deliberately, choosing your words carefully
- Walk slowly, purposefully and upright
- Practice active listening
- Light a candle or start a fire and sit in silence
- Forgive someone today
- Be present in the moment free of all distractions

Conclusion

"The feminine energy is a powerful force that is both nurturing and creative, a beautiful combination of strength and grace. It embodies love, beauty, and sensuality, and is a force to be reckoned with when harnessed with intention."

YOU ARE A SWEET, SEXY, BADASS QUEEN

Congratulations on making it till the end. You have learned about how to embody the sweet, kind Mother. You have discovered how to bring back your zest for life and take care of your inner girl and be a sexy Playmate. You have allowed your badass CEO to direct the outer world to accomplish all you require to live a successful life. And you have learned how to connect with the unshakeable, unbreakable power within your inner High Priestess to become the Queen. You have all you need to live a beautiful full life simply by calling on the part you require in any moment.

This is a dance, a dance between all archetypes. It is not a balance. I do not believe it is possible to achieve balance in life nor is it desirable. The reason I do not believe balance is possible is because when you look at a balance, both sides have to be equal. The balance is static and there is no movement on either side. If we try to say I want to balance all four Feminine types, you are talking about all four being equal in strength, in weight, in time, and in presence in your life. That is not going to give you fulfillment and power that you desire in your life.

Embodying the four Feminine types is more akin to a dance. Within any moment, when we are present and attuned to our mind, our heart, our bodies and our soul, we can dance with each energy. They are all dancing together giving us that sense of strength, power and fulfillment. Sometimes you move forward, sometimes you move backwards. Sometimes, you lead, sometimes you follow. There may seem no rhyme or reason on the outside, but each step is carefully orchestrated yet flowing. You are fully present with a knowledge of where you came from and what your next move will be. There is a powerful presence. You are in flow. You are 100% focused on what is present with a peripheral view of everything and everyone around you. In the present, your children may need your Mother's nurturing energy. That is not the time to crank up your Playmate. When faced with danger, you turn down your sexuality and lead with your CEO to get out of harm's way and be ready to fight, run or stand your ground. In a heated business meeting, you may not want to show your nurturing side which may be construed as vulnerability. Being present in the moment, allows an evolved woman to dance between all her Feminine types and access the required strengths as she needs them.

CREATING A MOVEMENT

In the depths of every woman lies a queen. A Sweet, Sexy, Badass Queen, to be exact. But how many of us are truly in touch with every aspect of ourselves? How often do we let our inner CEO take control in moments of decision-making? Or tap into our High Priestess when we're feeling spiritually adrift? And how often do we allow ourselves to indulge in playful, carefree moments as our inner Playmate craves?

Enter the movement of discovering and awakening the Sweet, Sexy, Badass Queen within. It's a journey of self-discovery, of recognizing the multifaceted nature of womanhood, and of embracing every single part of ourselves. No more suppressing certain aspects in favor of others. No more feeling ashamed or guilty for certain desires or tendencies.

The beauty of this movement lies in its simplicity. It's as easy as calling her in. Need to tackle a challenging project at work? Bring in your inner CEO. Feeling lost and in need of guidance? Call upon your High Priestess. Want to let loose and have some fun? Let your inner Playmate take the reins.

This movement is a reminder that every woman is a complex, dynamic being with a multitude of qualities and strengths to draw upon. It's an invitation to embrace our full selves and to live life with intention and purpose. So go ahead, call in your Sweet, Sexy, Badass Queen. She's ready and waiting for you to let her shine.

GODDESS MEDITATION

Take a deep breath and close your eyes. Place your feet flat on the ground and say hello to all four feminine archetypes. Imagine a four-leaf clover in front of you and notice what the Mother looks like at the top right-hand corner. Notice what the Playmate looks like on the bottom right-hand corner of the four-leaf clover. Notice what the CEO looks like on the bottom left-hand corner and what the High Priestess looks like on the top left.

Go ahead and release that four-leaf clover and allow yourself to bring in the energy of each of the feminine types. Above your head, create a big gold sun. Say hello to your inner Mother. What does your Mother energy look like? Bring that into the golden sun. Notice what color it comes in on. For me, it comes in on pink.

Then your Playmate, notice what color that Playmate comes in on. Just bring that into your sun. For me, it's a vibrant orange. If I want to have fun, I wear orange. Next, take a look at your inner CEO, your warrior energy, It's not something you have to look for outside, this is something you already have. Notice what color that comes in on. For me, it comes in on a beautiful turquoise blue color.

Finally, look at that High Priestess. It's a beautiful vibrant gold for me. Notice your color and fill up your sun with that High Priestess color. Watch that golden sun call back your essence. When that golden sun is all filled up, start to bring that down into your body, fill up all the spaces in your body and in your aura. Really receive all of that radiance. Receive back your energy that you might have left in other places, given away, denied, or blocked. Fill up completely all the way down to the tips of your toes.

Imagine a cord from a little bit below your seat that runs along your spine and comes up the top of your head. Straighten out that cord. You might give it a little tug because as goddesses, we all need to stand up a little taller. We all stand up a little straighter because we know who we are. We know what our divine essence is. We're able to enjoy life 110%. We're able to give out of a full, loving place. We're able to receive. We're able to make things happen in the world and create on a very powerful level. And we're always connected to our own truth, our own answers and our own divinity. Just stand up taller, no more slouching needed. We stand in our power, in our strength, in our beauty, in our divinity.

Afterword

When a woman embodies her full essence of the sweet, sexy, badass queen, she radiates with a confidence and grace that commands attention. She knows her worth, she knows her power, and she uses it to create the life she desires. Her beauty comes from within, from a deep place of self-love and self-acceptance. She honors her sensuality, her strength, and her intuition, and she fearlessly steps into her power to create a world that reflects her highest vision. She is a force to be reckoned with, and she inspires all those around her to do the same."

We live in exciting times for women. In developed countries, women have found more ways to achieve financial security, career opportunity, and freedom within families and we face fewer man-made limitations to reach our dreams. Women now want to have it all, be it all and do it all. In some ways, they emulate men to rise to the top within corporate and government structures. Using masculine energy, many get big offices, big jobs, and big money and many succeed in one way or another.

At the same time, women still hold onto the many roles and responsibilities apportioned to them. The fact is that while women can hold the corporate jobs and run their businesses, they are still the primary caretaker of the home and children. They work harder and longer than their counterparts. The question then becomes: How do we encompass all of it? How do we bring it all together so that we as women can strive for success and happiness while still feeling empowered at the end of the day, rather than depleted?

While this book doesn't seek to unravel the amazing advances made by women and for women, it hopefully put light on an unintended consequence of it, where women have swung to the opposite side of the pendulum and worked themselves to exhaustion. It proposes remedies for women, who in this modern age in which they bring home the bacon and also fry it, are simply fried out. Women who are power players in a man's world often feel exhausted, depleted, unhappy, and even depressed. They have lost touch with their femininity and have often lost themselves in others.

As a Business and Personal Coach and Strategist with over three decades of experience, I have counseled many of them. My clients come from all walks of life with income and status that run the spectrum. We talk about their relationships with men, their relationships with work and their understanding of real success and true happiness. My experience has helped me immensely, to develop a set of adjustments in our outlook and thinking, to counter the distress created when women find themselves having to operate like a man in a man's world.

I have helped many women get their "sexy" back, learn to gracefully manage their lives, and feel full of life at the end of the day, rather than exhausted and empty. They have been able to manifest their dreams, live their dream life, attract love, resources and success beyond their wildest imagination. And they wake up each day with a zest for life.

My prayer is that you receive the same blessings. That you too learn that you are indeed worth it. That you can have an incredible relationship where a real man can connect and protect you in such a way that makes you feel cherished and adored. I want you to have the successful career, feel beautiful in your skin, and feel connected to the deepest part of your inner being.

My goal is to show you how you can have it all, be it all and do it all. I promise you, it is not only possible, but absolutely probable. Congratulations on the start of your Sweet, Sexy, Badass and Queenly journey of life long transformation!

With love to your beautiful journey,
Trez

Acknowledgements

No project ever comes to fruition without the guidance, love and support of the people around you; the people that believe in you, the ones that cheer you on and the ones that provide the emotional and logistical support and guidance that make the earth move. I have been blessed to have many such people in my life, and for that, I am eternally grateful. My only fear is leaving out those who have had an impact on my life and supported me on my journey to living the best life I can live.

My greatest love and gratitude go to my parents, who left this earth plane at such a young age but who have left an indelible mark on my heart and a desire and drive to live my dreams, love my life and share kindness everywhere I go. Their unconditional love towards me is something I strive to emulate every day. Mom and dad, I know you are in heaven and have been watching me grow and I pray that you are proud of the woman you have guided me to become.

To my beloved son, whom I love more than words can say. You have been the light of my life, and a constant source of joy and inspiration. You have been with me through thick and thin, and your unwavering love and support have sustained me during the toughest times. As I wrote this book, I thought of you often and how much I want you to grow up in a world where women are empowered, valued, and respected. You have shown me what it means to be a true man – one who is strong, protective, kind, compassionate, and supportive of the women in his life. I am so proud of the person you have become and the man you are growing into.

To my chosen sisters, Angela and Helen, my ride-or-dies, my partners in crime, thank you for being my rock, my laughter, my love, and my light. Your unwavering support and encouragement mean the world to me. I love you both so much. I don't know how I could have made the last 45 years without you both by my side. Thank you for the friendship, the love, the laughter, and the wonderful adventures. I look forward to the next 45 years with you and many more wonderful escapades.

I also want to express my gratitude to all the mentors, teachers, coaches, and guides who have inspired me, challenged me, and helped me to become the best version of myself. Your teachings have played an invaluable role in shaping my life and this book. Thank you for showing me the true meaning of dedication and passion. Your unwavering commitment to your craft has motivated me to strive for excellence every single day.

To all my clients, past, present, and future, thank you for showing me the power of perseverance, determination, and resilience. Your growth and progress inspire me to keep pushing forward, and I am honored to have been a part of your journey.

Lastly, to all those who have supported me along the way. Dina, who has put so much work into getting this book ready for publication and has been a god send in my life. Thank you for supporting me so I can support others. To my friends, colleagues and partners, know that your love and encouragement have not gone unnoticed. Thank you for being a part of my life and for helping me to become the woman and teacher I am today.

With love and gratitude,
Trez

About the Author

Trez Ibrahim is an Evolutionary Strategist, Spiritual Catalyst and Master Success Coach. Trained in Neuro-Change, Emotional Release, Energy Work, and Business and Organizational Development, she has been working with some of the most prominent business owners, executives, entrepreneurs and organizations in the world for over 30 years to help them reach massive levels of success.

She believes that to be truly Full-filled, you need to be living at a 10 in every area of your life. . . having the career that makes you jump out of bed each morning, making the money that supports your desired life style, having the free time to enjoy your life, being in optimal health to get through your day with energy and vitality, and having supportive loving relationships with deep and meaningful connection.

She has authored 4 books, worked with fortune 50 companies and is an international transformational thought leader. She co-creates with her clients, using manifestation techniques most "gurus" miss, releasing limiting beliefs and decisions, healing old emotional baggage, releasing internal and external conflict, and creating new life-thriving habits to Live A Life By Design.

She lives in Southern California, loves to travel and enjoy the present moment with all the magic and miracles it has to offer.

Made in the USA
Las Vegas, NV
17 January 2024

84479851R00152